RACE AND NEW MODERNISMS

NEW MODERNISMS SERIES

Bloomsbury's *New Modernisms* series introduces, explores, and extends the major topics and debates at the forefront of contemporary Modernist Studies.

Surveying new engagements with such topics as race, sexuality, technology, and material culture, and supported with authoritative further reading guides to the key works in contemporary scholarship, these books are essential guides for serious students and scholars of Modernism.

Published Titles

Modernism: Evolution of an Idea, Sean Latham and Gayle Rogers

Modernism and the Law, Robert Spoo

Modernism in a Global Context, Peter J. Kalliney

Modernism's Print Cultures, Faye Hammill and Mark Hussey

Modernism, Science, and Technology, Mark S. Morrisson

Modernism, Sex, and Gender, Celia Marshik and Allison Pease

Modernism, War, and Violence, Marina MacKay

Race and Modernisms, K. Merinda Simmons and James A. Crank

Forthcoming Titles

Modernism and Its Environments, Michael Rubenstein and Justin Neuman

The Global Avant-Garde, Christopher Bush

Modernism and Its Media, Chris Forster

RACE AND NEW MODERNISMS

K. MERINDA SIMMONS
AND JAMES A. CRANK

BLOOMSBURY ACADEMIC
LONDON • NEW YORK • OXFORD • NEW DELHI • SYDNEY

BLOOMSBURY ACADEMIC
Bloomsbury Publishing Plc
50 Bedford Square, London, WC1B 3DP, UK
1385 Broadway, New York, NY 10018, USA

BLOOMSBURY, BLOOMSBURY ACADEMIC and the Diana logo are
trademarks of Bloomsbury Publishing Plc

First published in Great Britain 2019

Copyright © K. Merinda Simmons and James A. Crank, 2019

For legal purposes the Acknowledgments on p. viii constitute an extension
of this copyright page.

Cover design: Daniel Benneworth-Gray
Cover photograph © Paul Robeson leading Moore Shipyard workers in
singing the Star-Spangled Banner, 1942

A catalogue record for this book is available from the British Library.

Library of Congress Cataloging-in-Publication Data
Names: Simmons, Merinda, 1981- author. | Crank, James A., author.
Title: Race and new modernisms / K. Merinda Simmons and James A. Crank.
Description: London; New York, NY A: Bloomsbury Academic, 2019. |
Includes bibliographical references. Identifiers: LCCN 2019002251|
ISBN 9781350030404 (hb) | ISBN 9781350030398 (pb)
Subjects: LCSH: Race in literature. | Ethnicity in literature. |
Literature, Modern—History and criticism.
Classification: LCC PN56.R16 S57 2019 | DDC 809/.933552–dc23 LC record
available at https://lccn.loc.gov/2019002251

ISBN: HB: 978-1-3500-3040-4
PB: 978-1-3500-3039-8
ePDF: 978-1-3500-3042-8
eBook: 978-1-3500-3041-1

Series: New Modernisms

Typeset by Deanta Global Publishing Services, Chennai, India
Printed and bound in Great Britain

To find out more about our authors and books visit www.bloomsbury.com
and sign up for our newsletters.

for Arlo

CONTENTS

ACKNOWLEDGMENTS

This book project received generous support from multiple sources, and we are very grateful to all who made it possible. First, we would very much like to thank the College of Arts and Sciences, the Department of English, and the Department of Religious Studies at the University of Alabama—each of these units provided financial assistance and professional encouragement during the process of this book's composition. Very special thanks to administrators and colleagues Bob Olin, Tricia McElroy, Joel Brouwer, and Russell McCutcheon. We had the extremely good fortune to complete this manuscript at the National Humanities Center in Durham, NC. The people who coordinated and facilitated our stay in the summer of 2018—especially Lynn Miller, Brooke Andrade, Sarah Harris, and Joel Elliott—are extraordinary, and we are grateful to National Humanities Center (NHC) director Robert Newman. This book is indebted to the NHC's beautiful spaces, library support, and endless coffee.

Our editors, Gayle Rogers and Sean Latham, have been wonderful resources, both intellectually and collegially. They—along with David Avital and Clara Herberg at Bloomsbury Academic—have our deepest thanks.

From Andy: I have wonderful friends and family (biological and chosen) who have helped me in more ways than I can say; first and always is Jeff (every book is yours); Phyllis and Bill Agnew; Dad, Shelly, Steve, Don, Daniel Crank; always-Abbie; Nathan, Arlo; Memorie, Joe,

Sam, Tucker; Samantha Hansen; Mark Hernandez, Cristian Asher, Dean Skiles; Heidi Norwood; Erich Nunn and Amy Clukey (the band); Michael Bibler and the whole Society for the Study of Southern Literature (SSSL) crew; Kate, Layton, and Joshua Whitman; Wendy Rawlings, Trudier Harris, David Deutsch, and Sharon Holland; my phenomenal students; my family of friends that I have been stuncle to; special thanks to Carol and Mr. Excitement and the staff/crew of the Alamo Drafthouse in Raleigh and China Palace in Durham; always, of course, Maddie, forever and ever, amen. This book has benefited from one amazing graduate student, who worked with me to compile bibliographies, edit, and work through indices. Thank you so much Sarah Landry! And, finally, but most significantly, my undying love and gratitude go to one K. Merinda Simmons (aka Mlubz): working with my best friend in the world on a project about which we both feel passionate and invested has been one of the greatest joys of my professional life. Thanks for taking me with you.

From Merinda: For helping see this book through to completion, I am especially indebted to my colleagues in the Department of Religious Studies at UA, to Becky Brown for her careful eye, to the inimitable Andy Crank, and to my beloveds: Nathan and Arlo. Always, and most especially, my very warmest thanks go to Houston A. Baker, Jr., whose work has made generations of important analyses possible, and to the amazing Charlotte Pierce-Baker, an unlimited resource of insight, wisdom, humor, and kindness. Houston, thank you for being, among so many other things, the voice in my head.

Introduction—Coming to Terms: Identifying Race and New Modernisms

Just thirteen years short of a century after it was written, Zora Neale Hurston's first book *Barracoon: The Story of the Last "Black Cargo"* was finally published in 2018. In it, Hurston introduces Cudjo Lewis (born Oluale Kossola), one of the last-known survivors of the Atlantic slave trade. Captured by warriors from a neighboring tribe, Kossola and over one hundred others were sold into slavery and taken on the *Clotilda* to Alabama's coast in 1860. After the Civil War and after he could raise enough money to buy some land, Kossola became one of the founders of Africatown, just north of Mobile, where inhabitants were able to maintain West African languages and traditions. Hurston transcribed interviews with Kossola that would become the basis for *Barracoon*, ultimately finishing the book in 1931. However, she failed to secure a publisher, as she insisted on telling his story in written dialect and on grappling directly with Africans' roles in the Atlantic slave trade.

The eventual publication of the book may seem like an obvious and overdue posthumous gesture, but canon is a slippery and contingent concept. After all, while Hurston worked and wrote among other luminaries of the Harlem Renaissance, she was anything but a conventional figure in the literary scene. Never shying away from controversy, she committed to reproducing as faithfully as she could the voices of black southerners who populated her work. Richard Wright famously railed against *Their Eyes Were Watching God* (1937), chastising what he saw to be a perpetuation of black stereotypes on the order of minstrelsy. What's more, Hurston spent the final years of her life in obscurity, ultimately being buried in an unmarked grave. She did not gain the status that has come to appear obvious to present-day readers until the 1970s, when Alice Walker brought her works back into the light of day with her *Ms.* Magazine article "In Search of Our Mothers' Gardens: The Creativity of Black Women in the South" and then with her 1983 book by the same name (but with the broader subtitle, *Womanist Prose*)—now canonical works in their own right. Almost as well known as Hurston's work is Walker's reintroduction of it, her journey to Florida to locate and mark Hurston's grave (an endeavor of approximation by necessity). At the very least, any substantive consideration of the Harlem Renaissance figure in relation to her eventual readership and prominence is necessarily also a rendering of Walker's project in its own context of womanism's entrée into cultural discourse and second-wave feminist publishing.

Fittingly, Alice Walker wrote *Barracoon*'s foreword, another introduction some forty-five years after locating the unmarked grave that she attributed to Hurston. In those prefatory pages, Walker draws attention to, among other things, the book's straightforward depiction of the buying and selling of Africans by other Africans—one that, along with the stylistic license with dialect, made prospective publishers balk at the project in the early 1930s. That Hurston's first book is a contemporary advent, then, should not be seen as an arbitrary bit of literary happenstance. Nor should it be seen as an inevitability of universally agreed-upon authorial genius. The now certain status of Hurston's authorial place in the pantheon of black modernists—and the grave-marker moniker offered by Walker, "Genius of the South"—was not at all a stable or sure outcome.

Hurston as a literary and cultural figure presents a conundrum for her readers and scholars, just as she did for her contemporaries. She is at once a figure of the Harlem Renaissance and the Southern Renaissance. She was independently minded and a traditionalist, an anthropologist and a novelist, a lightning rod who nonetheless died in relative obscurity. Within a cultural context of racial uplift that announced the creative artistry of the New Negro, Hurston was a conservative—a critic of communism and an advocate of Booker T. Washington's vision of African American self-sufficiency—who nonetheless advanced feminist themes that certainly did not enjoy a mainstream presence among her contemporaries' politics of racial progress. In this way, Hurston's presence in the Harlem Renaissance canon is also an absence. Politically and ideologically, she was a fringe figure among other writers who rallied around a form of black identitarian politics befitting modern sensibilities that aimed to gather a foothold on the American ladder of upward mobility and economic advancement. Hers is also a story of temporal shifts and simultaneities—her first book of the last cargo would be her last published, and it would be read only in the next century. Her eventual reintroduction by Alice Walker arrives at the nexus of aesthetics, economic access and disenfranchisement, structural racism, and ideas about ancestry.

Hurston's life and work collapsed the would-be boundary between aesthetics and politics in ways that reveal a sort of Möbius strip of modernism and race. The proximity of these two categories has never been one of artistic expression alone, nor was it about an ostensibly pure ideology. Hurston was also intent on making her own aesthetic point, often to the chagrin of her contemporaries who were invested in showcasing a particular brand of race politics with their work. Such contradictions and simultaneous discourses—of canon, access, philosophy, politics, writing, and timing—are what we will suggest have always been present in the relationship between race and modernism. These simultaneities and crosscurrents are what we aim to address in this book, emphasizing not the *what* but the *how* of race, modernism, and the cultural products therein.

There is a core problem of terminology in any exploration of modernism within the framework of race/racial identification. The very concept of modernism makes little sense without the coextensive identifications of race that have implicitly and explicitly attended it. Consequently, our approach throughout this book relies upon an understanding of "race" and "modernism" that sees the terms as interlocking conceptual tools instead of separate spheres of descriptive analysis. This approach might appear self-evident, especially after the post-structuralist critical turn. However, we want not only to engage the connections between the terms but also to explore the tenuous gaps between the words, especially considering the current scholarly conversations surrounding "new modernisms."

Prior to the shift away from a conventional definition of modernism—one that remained fairly static over several decades of literary and cultural criticism—the debates surrounding modernist texts, authors, and histories largely looked at race as an aesthetic concern. Major figures in modernist studies such as Michael North and Marjorie Perloff emphasized race and racial identification as tools through which (largely white) authors explored the complex markers of identification that they would come to trouble in their work. For those scholars, "race" functioned as a medium in modernist texts for themes of fragmentation, disillusionment, and alienation. With analytical interventions that challenged scholars to push further the idea of race as a rhetorical move rather than a biological phenomenon, more room was made for the reaches of this idea as it took shape in other fields and from other perspectives. This "new modernist" turn—in concert with a broader transnational turn in American and cultural studies in general—offered a dynamic potential for the field that called for greater scholarly self-awareness in relation to race and subjectivity.

What has been called new modernist studies began to shift the conversation away from the limits and boundaries of modernism as a movement associated with the fantasies, desires, and psychologies of white authors and to expand the field by broadening the focus beyond singular definitions of texts, authors, artists, dialogues, movements, histories, and people. Thus, the new modernist studies embraced the enormous mesh of possibilities contained in thinking beyond the limitations of fixed places and ideas. A central element of new modernisms involved attending to the political and structural (rather than aesthetic) dynamics that shaped modernist conceptions of "race" and to how these dynamics evolved as a result of those conceptions. Taking these contextual forces into account allowed for more careful considerations of how a "modernist perspective" identified race in ways that have both constituted and complicated the pursuit (aesthetically or analytically) of that very perspective. Thus, we are not so much interested in discussing "race" and "modernism" as such— as stable things *out there* existing in the world—in order to offer a descriptive or comprehensive history (neither of which is possible anyway). Instead, we will discuss the kinds of debates that became crucibles for identifying and operationalizing race and modernism in various contexts.

New modernism(s)

To employ a phrase like "new modernism," or to refer to this book as a part of a larger project of "new modernist studies," implies that there was an "old modernism" or, at the very least, an ending to a critical apparatus and the birth of a new one surrounding the very concept of "the modern." Such a binary about the study of modernism doesn't quite work. Indeed, talking in any way about a monolithic "modern" object or text or work of art becomes antithetical to the very tension scholarly moves that came to be thought of as constituting a new modernist trend have sought to address. This book not only examines how narratives of and about race operate in modernist texts but also acknowledges the reflexive practices that have and continue to open the field of modernism. These practices have been aimed at addressing multiple kinds of texts, articulations, and subjects—especially inasmuch as multiplicity was always present for modernist figures like Hurston, for whom analyses identifying singularity or an irreducible quality simply do not work. But first, perhaps, we should address the two key markers of the phrase itself: What exactly is so "new" and "modern" about new modernism(s), and how do these approaches invite plurality and deny singularity?

Origin narratives seem always to be born of fantasy and myth, but when critics want to put a specific date on the "birth" of new modernist studies, they generally point to the decade of the 1990s, for two specific reasons: 1994 was when the journal *Modernism/modernity* began its run, and 1998/1999 saw the formation of the Modernist Studies Association. Critics in the 1990s realized the crisis of conflation that modernism had become, but more importantly, they recognized its limited utility in a time of expansive study. At a time when gender, sexuality, ethnicity, and race studies were being formalized on campuses across the globe, modernism remained doggedly entrenched in its own self-referential and limited definitions of identity. In short, there were more integers and exciting multiplications to investigate, but modernist critics seemed to want to stick to their simplistic paradigms of addition/subtraction and to the work of tending their own gardens.

In 2006, Douglas Mao and Rebecca L. Walkowitz published their important quasi-jeremiad *Bad Modernisms*, which sought to take the field to task for its recalcitrance and stubborn navel gazing. Mao and Walkowitz argued that any modernism that constituted an exploration of the field's conventional emphasis on the ahistorical and apolitical love of the aesthetic was "bad" and needed to be disciplined. Writing in *PMLA* a few years after the publication of *Bad Modernisms*,

Mao and Walkowitz sought further to distance themselves from the understanding of modernism as, in the words of Majorie Perloff, "a retrograde, elitist movement" (2006, 154):

> For many years modernism was understood as, precisely, a movement by and for a certain kind of high (cultured mandarins) as against a certain kind of low (the masses, variously regarded as duped by the "culture industry," admirably free of elitist self-absorption, or simply awaiting the education that would make the community of cognoscenti a universal one). (2008, 738)

Instead, Mao and Walkowitz imagined a field that would be, in keeping with the energy of the decade, one that embraced the array of possibilities that academic inquiry privileged: "Were one seeking a single word to sum up transformations in modernist literary scholarship over the past decade or two, one could do worse than light on *expansion*" (2008, 737, emphasis in original), they offered. New modernist studies was presented first and foremost as an expansive field of study.

In their introduction to *Bad Modernisms*, Mao and Walkowitz argue that the "cultural producers hitherto seen as neglecting or resisting modernist innovation" have slowly begun to seep into the field, as have the "fusion of theoretical commitments" (1–2) and the desire to explore the relationships between individual works of art and their broader cultural contexts. Embracing new fields, foci, authors, artists, cultures, and theoretical paradigms help to define what was "new" about this new emphasis within the larger field. As part of their charge to their fellow critics, Mao and Walkowitz also encouraged scholars to examine the long history of modernism itself in order that they might "bring forgotten badness to light" (7) and disarticulate theoretical models that refused to engage with broader contexts in favor of establishing and entrenching ideological positions. Of course, one difficulty with this new modernist turn in the field was organizing it around one central thematic or heuristic. The very mission of a new modernist studies resisted monoliths and singularity.

Mao and Walkowitz saw the expansion of the field in three distinct trajectories, "temporal, spatial, and vertical" (737). New modernist scholars would inevitably—and rightfully—question the rigidness of time periods used to describe a modernist agenda, ultimately settling on a more flexible and open definition of what constitutes the work of modernism. Spatial concerns of modernism would attempt to remove the focus of scholars from the conventional terrain of Europe and North America and instead attend to other cultures, peoples, nations, ethnicities, and languages. And, finally, Mao and Walkowitz found value in the idea of a reassessment of modernism from the top down:

> In addition to these temporal and spatial expansions, there has been what we are calling here a vertical one, in which quite sharp boundaries between high art and popular forms of culture have been reconsidered; in which canons have been critiqued and reconfigured; in which works by members of marginalized social groups have been encountered with fresh eyes and ears; and in which scholarly inquiry has increasingly extended to matters of production, dissemination, and reception. (737–38)

This approach necessitated a reconsideration of terminology. If scholars had been simply pulling at strands in an intricate tapestry— if there was no monolithic modernism, no constituency or nation or region that owned the term—they could also acknowledge that the field itself is primarily interested in an investigation of plurality.

All the same, we suggest, plurality alone (or the pluralizing of "modernisms") is not an end in itself and should not be thought to do analytical heavy lifting in its own right. A thoroughgoing investigation of the concept of modernism—the people who have deployed it and the sites and implications of those deployments, including contemporary scholarly moments—is necessary if the pluralizing of the term is to carry any substantive critical weight. This project endeavors to offer such an investigation, examining the slippages and tensions between "race" and modernist representations of the same. Our chapters will examine sites and contexts wherein, in the service of modernist projects, identifications of race were coextensive with ideas about modernism even as the former complicated the latter and vice versa. We will highlight some of the major figures of the literary/artistic historical moment we explore in each chapter, as well as major critical figures who have helped shape the discussion of the movement we're addressing. Doing so with an eye toward not "the thing itself" but rather discourse *about* the thing, we emphasize the scholarly conversations about *x* or *y* more than we do the primary texts. This is a deliberate move aimed at casting our discussion within the larger framework of new modernist studies, reflecting on its possibilities and limitations along the way. Thus, while we will investigate conventionally and classically modernist texts and figures, we will do so through a critical lens that will allow us to think through these conventionally modernist moments in new ways and with new outcomes. We do not seek to entrench further any modernist moments, but wish instead to interrogate what has traditionally received representation within these conversations about race and modernism. Presenting at the beginning of each chapter a few guiding questions that open up in broad terms the discussion to follow, we proceed through considerations of some critical concepts that we find significant to the context in question.

Race: Classifications and contingencies

The attempts of writers, artists, and performers to place their endeavors in relation to something called modernism were never without fraught racial implications and positionalities. Ezra Pound's praising T. S. Eliot for having "modernized himself *on his own*," for example, offers an occasion to think about what was presumed as part of this individualist ideal (*Selected Letters* 40, emphasis in original). The capacity for such an entrepreneurial modernist project, of course, is impossible without the privileges attendant in a particular racial, economic, and masculinist position. Eliot's "mind of Europe," to which he appealed as a signifier of literary greatness/tradition, poses another similar analytical exercise ("Tradition" 6). Making plain the assumptions and ideologies that needed to be in place in order to build what became modernist canon is part of the scholarly turn that discontinued accepting modernism as an aesthetic enterprise alone and instead began taking serious stock of the contextual power dynamics that shaped a piece of art deemed "modernist." Indeed, these recent turns have been pivotal in deconstructing the notion of a pure aesthetic at all, revealing modernism to be a rhetorical and ideological possibility only because of these imbrications in the first place. Houston A. Baker, Jr. noted as much in 1987 at the beginning of his classic *Modernism and the Harlem Renaissance*: "Promising a wealth of meaning, [the term 'modernism'] locks observers into a questing indecision that can end in unctuous chiasmus" (1).

Thinking about race and new modernism with any utility, then, is an exercise in taking seriously the sites where these two classifications became performed and contested. These debates, of course, have always been wound up in modernist discourse, and it would be a mistake to identify such concerns as a phenomenon unique to scholarly moves since the advent of identity studies after the 1970s. One need only look to the investments revealed in disputes over regional dialect and racial uplift during the Harlem Renaissance. Alain Locke's popularizing of a post–First World War "New Negro" who demanded self-determination and social respectability/mobility, for example, was as much aesthetic as it was political. Black writers, artists, and musicians fashioned new modes of African American expressive and material culture, while direct political action took shape in (among other things, like configurations of an urban black metropolis in northern cities) Marcus Garvey's Pan-Africanist call for the African diaspora to abandon American societal constraints and reclaim their homelands by returning to Africa. Despite its broad applications, however, the New Negro archetype did not remain uncontested. Novelist and essayist Wallace Thurman, for example, famously argued in several of his works (including his 1932 novel *Infants of Spring*) that the movement lacked cohesion and ultimately continued to rely upon white patronage (and implicit exploitation). In his review of Locke's 1925 representative anthology of creative and intellectual works,

The New Negro, Thurman suggests, "Many have wondered what this Negro literary renaissance has accomplished other than provide white publishers with a new source of revenue, affording the white intellectuals with a 'different' fad and bringing a half dozen Negro artists out of obscurity" (qtd. in van Notten, 103). Cofounder of the National Negro Congress John P. Davis was another who criticized the movement, arguing that Locke had failed to offer concrete mechanisms by which to operationalize his lofty ideals.

Inasmuch as race is, as Nell Irvin Painter (2010) succinctly wrote, "an idea, not a fact," the concept as it coalesced for Locke and his contemporaries was very different from other iterations and connotations. Historically speaking, the terms "race" and "species" were more or less synonymous into the 1700s. Thus, to talk about a different race was to talk of something entirely distinct from the humanity invoked in Enlightenment thought. Enlightenment emphases on reason and scientific empiricism were, of course, nonetheless in the service of imperial efforts and a narrative of European exceptionalism. Alongside an interest in investigating "the natural world"—as opposed to appealing to theistic explanations— was an interest in Western "civilization" and the question of how to think and talk about groups encountered during European colonial projects. The term "race" underwent massive overhauls as recently as the eighteenth and nineteenth centuries when those imperial endeavors were at their zenith, such that, by the early twentieth century, the concept of "race" was inextricably linked to—indeed, often used synonymously with—nation. By extension, Jewish, Irish, and Italian immigrants in the United States, for example, were not understood to be "white."

Approaches to race had long moved past the species-speak of Enlightenment thinking but retained intellectual holdovers from the time period, identifying race as an essence whose meaning goes unchanged across contexts. Modernist writers represented and articulated critiques of this partial progress. In their essay "The Theoretical Status of the Concept of Race" (2005), Michael Omi and Howard Winant point to thinkers who began to dislodge race from biological fixity in the early decades of the twentieth century, such as W. E. B. Du Bois, Franz Boas, and Robert E. Park—along with "racial theorists emerging from the intellectual and cultural ferment of the Negritude movement and the Harlem Renaissance, pan-Africanists and nationalists, and Marxists electrified by the Russian revolution" (2005, 3). The theory of "racial formation" (emphasizing the ways in which race is socially constructed) that Omi and Winant put forward in 1986 was a precursor to a new modernist studies and would consider race in similar terms. Seeing acts of naming as a complex social web of interrelated networks of power rather than as a neutral or passive act of description, these approaches would make significant moves forward in emphasizing the dynamism of race and modernism, of politics and aesthetics.

These themes and debates came to be revived in various ways in the scholarship that would take up race and modernism as key elements of an early twentieth-century dialectic regarding identity and society. Paul Gilroy's *The Black Atlantic: Modernity and Double-Consciousness* (1993) was part of the work heralding the kind of analysis that would come to be called "new modernism." His emphasis on a transatlantic mode of acculturation attempts to complicate erstwhile singularities of cultural development and experience, be they Caribbean, American, African, or British. A decade later, in *The Practice of Diaspora* (2003), Brent Hayes Edwards would build upon and complicate Gilroy's approach further by bringing France into the conversation about cultural exchange and by discussing diaspora as a set of practices rather than discrete geospatial movements or historical moments. The New Negro movement, as Edwards demonstrates, was simultaneously a new black internationalism, infused with systems of translation, correspondence, and collaboration. The year 2003 also saw the publication of Laura Chrisman's *Postcolonial Contraventions*, which devotes a chapter to Gilroy's black Atlantic formulation. In Chrisman's view, the brand of nationalism Gilroy theorizes collapses diverse performances of nation and identity, painting white and black communities with the same, far-too-broad brush. Scholars like Catherine Hall (1992) and Vron Ware (1992), meanwhile, critique the androcentric nature of Gilroy's work, noting the absence of women (e.g., abolitionist-era figures like Ida B. Wells and Charlotte Grimke) who were pivotal in the processes of exchange outlined in *The Black Atlantic*. Further, as Robert Reid-Pharr (1994) has pointed out, black nationalism as outlined by thinkers like Du Bois was never too far removed from black patriarchy.

Other scholarly works from the mid-1990s—such as Walter Benn Michaels's *Our America: Nativism, Modernism, and Pluralism* (1995) and Ann Douglas's *Terrible Honesty: Mongrel Manhattan in the 1920s* (1995)—share similar trajectories, delving into controversies over identity and multiculturalism in modernist contexts, only to become controversial texts themselves among scholarly communities. These debates prefigure recent turns in the field, which now attend to an array of emphases in order to think through broader implications of identity and performance (such as Monica Miller's *Slaves to Fashion: Dandyism and the Styling of Black Diasporic Identity* (2009), Ben Hutchinson's *Modernism and Style* (2011), William J. Maxwell's *New Negro, Old Left: African American Writing and Communism between the Wars* (1999), Donald J. Childs's *Modernism and Eugenics* (2001), and Michael Golston's *Rhythm and Race in Modernist Poetry and Science* (2007)).

These important trends and contestations rely, of course, on the work of pivotal scholarship that announced itself in the 1980s by way of questioning the very frameworks of the civilization (and critique thereof) on which modernist claims had relied on up to that point.[1] Houston Baker's aforementioned *Modernism and the Harlem Renaissance* (1987), for example, described the analytical conundrum like this: "It is difficult, for example, for an Afro-American student of literature like me—one unconceived in the philosophies of Anglo-American, British, and Irish moderns—to find intimacy either in the moderns' hostility to *civilization* or in their fawning reliance on an array of images and assumptions bequeathed by a *civilization* that, in its prototypical form, is exclusively Western, preeminently bourgeois, and optically white" (6).

Along with Baker's 1987 text, Henry Louis Gates, Jr's *The Signifying Monkey: A Theory of African-American Literary Criticism* (1988) made a vital intervention in both modernist studies and literary criticism. Theorizing the roles of linguistic particularity and improvisation, Baker and Gates offer readings of variance and the vernacular in black literature that situate African American discourse in such a way as to deconstruct the very notion of a high modernist canon. With the subversion of traditional formalism and a repositioning of aesthetics in relation to discursive performance and political action, a different timeline of modernist work and sensibilities emerged—one that began, in Baker's estimation, with Booker T. Washington's Atlanta Compromise speech in 1895 and ended, in Gates's view, with Ishmael Reed's 1972 novel *Mumbo Jumbo*. Importantly, these bookends provide cultural moments of both political and creative forms. In configurations of African American modernism, these modes have always been inextricably linked.

Creating a framework and paving the way for these foundational works was the institutionalization for the first time of black studies as a formal disciplinary pursuit in colleges and universities. The critiques of dominant authority structures that gave ideological voice to movements demanding racial equality and an end to war in the 1960s and 1970s played out in the academy as well. New programs and departments in black studies, Africana studies, and African American studies offered suggestive ways ahead for the antiauthoritarian intellectual strands that directed scholarly attention to "race" as an object of study in its own right. In these spaces, ignored histories began to see the light of day, and inroads were made into scholarly discourses up and running—among them, modernist studies.

The modernist canon, like any other, has historically been exclusionary in multiple ways, and new modernist moves have attempted to bring traditionally ignored texts by people of color into the discussion so as to take more accurate stock of the global reaches and implications of modernist ideology. As Latham and Rogers suggest, "it might be possible to see the history of modernism as a history of exclusions such as these and their interactions . . . with all that they attempted to occlude" (10). The merits and limits of representation as an end in itself, however, must be considered in the midst of increasing calls for a bigger tent. How does the incorporation of historically overlooked texts, writers, and artists allow for different and more substantive questions about the work of visibility? In what ways does such visibility rely upon traditional valuations of realism and humanism, the limits of which have recently come into focus for scholars trying to press forward the critical terms of engagement that have too long preoccupied modernist discourse? To what extent does representative subjectivity prove exclusionary in its own right, allowing a structural avoidance of a more thoroughgoing interrogation of how a canon is manufactured, of what politics and power dynamics are present in its formation? How might formations of new modernism that attend to these exclusions also take serious account of what Aaron Jaffe has called "intersectional repositioning for inhuman scales"?[2]

Looking at how "race" came to be formed and fashioned coextensively with discourses on a modernist tradition means examining the latter as thoroughly social and political endeavors rather than singularly aesthetic or ideational descriptions. That is, the very notion of "tradition" comes into relief as a racially inflected, sociopolitically loaded term. In a similar vein, we might ask who was able to assume power to consolidate tradition with access to those means. Doing so reveals "the modernist tradition" to be unavoidably wrapped up in power dynamics inflected by many factors, not the least of which was racial identification.

Similarly entrenched in the inescapable politics of classification are the critical moves over the second half of the twentieth century and into the twenty-first that "added an ever-growing collection of cultural filings that included works by black poets, subaltern artists, and those who wrote or worked beyond, in only tangential relation to, or even with contempt for, Eliot's 'European mind'" (Latham and Rogers, 10). New modernism builds upon this process by considering, for example, contemporary displacements of and crises for immigrant and refugee communities in light of and as extensions of the ways in which citizenship and nation-state boundaries came to be legislated in the modernist period.

This study: Collapsing aesthetics and politics

Inasmuch as we consider self-reflexivity a hallmark of constructive scholarship, we find it worthwhile to think through at the outset some of this book's structural elements before launching into its finer points. Case in point: our title. While *Race and New Modernisms* may appear at first blush to be straightforward enough, simply identifying a topic easily surveyed with relevant figures and events, the phrasing is worth considering. There are significant theoretical moves that have to be made and kept up and running for the pairing offered in this volume's title to be centered as a conceptual moniker in the first place—as if "race" and "modernisms" are passive descriptions rather than suggestive rhetorical tools. Indeed, the conjunction "and" does a great deal of work from the outset. Namely, it implicitly points to two separate domains of social phenomena. If they intersect or affect each other at certain points, that may become its own particular discussion, but each is seen as discernable from the other. There is *this* and there is *that*. More apt, we suggest, would be to talk about how these processes of naming operate in relation to each other: how "race" comes to be fashioned in new modernist analyses, and how "modernism" itself was identified through racially inflected prisms proliferating in the rhetorics of civilization, nationhood, cosmopolitanism, and otherness. Doing so allows us to think about a figure like Zora Neale Hurston within the complex series of interlocking aesthetic and political dynamics in which she lived and wrote. Such an approach helps us to read her first book for the first time in 2018, to take stock of her intellectual pursuits in both anthropology and creative writing, and to consider in nuanced ways her conservative politics inside Harlem in the early years of the Great Migration and at the height of Jim Crow.

To that end, as stated above, each chapter of *Race and New Modernisms* outlines the matter being discussed through a handful of concepts (terms, ideas, and/or tropes) that offer useful ways in which to think through the topic at hand. These are meant to serve as neither descriptive nor foreclosing catalogs but rather as constructive analytical entrées—signposts for a careful reader to read broadly the key terms and phrases that animate the debate over each chapter's subject. Since our volume is more of a critical primer than a survey, the concepts provide important moments of our recognizing our own scholarly starting points in the midst of the inevitable work of historicizing various subjects. After all, there are myriad ways to talk about the complex relationships between "race and new modernisms."

Our own way in to talking about these relationships sustains a predominant focus on African diasporas and the modernist rhetorics in and about those contexts, especially as figured in the Americas and Europe. This emphasis reflects only a couple of, decidedly mundane, factors. Of course, there are the pragmatic constraints and inevitable exclusions of geolocating sites that allow for productive conversation about "race and new modernisms" within a single brief volume. Additionally, our examples reflect our own scholarly areas of research and writing. The foregrounding of black American, Caribbean, and European sites of analysis should in no way be read as suggesting that they are more important or exceptional than other contexts. Further, *because* African diasporas figure prominently in our other scholarship, we are all too aware of the frequent and frustrating conflation of race with "blackness." That the latter often serves as metonym for the former (not unlike the familiar phenomenon in which a discussion about "gender" is thought necessarily to be a discussion about "women") is an analytical failure to take seriously the roles of invisible norms, as well as shifting boundaries and borders of ever-evolving nation-states and the communities inside them.

These realities are very much in our minds as we embark on a discussion of how race became—indeed, had always implicitly been— embedded within the very concept of modernism, and vice versa. We begin, in Chapter 1, with the trope of the American expatriate in Europe, acknowledging its resonance for modernism writ large and examining its romanticizing of racial otherness. Taking a cue from Michael North's *The Dialect of Modernism: Race, Language, and Twentieth-Century Modernism* (1994), we will look at these artists and writers in relation to broader contexts. While North offers an incredibly compelling comparative study of writers in Europe and America, we will add to the discussion rhetorical and aesthetic configurations of Africa. We will also touch on an even greater global range for some of these issues that shared the coupling of exoticism and othering that typifies so much of the modernist obsession with primitivism.

Chapter 2 takes up the era after the abolition of slavery and the attendant anxiety over how to deal with economic and cultural investments in postcolonial spaces in the UK. With a focus on three specific sites: Haiti, Cuba, and Puerto Rico—colonies that become important for modernist fashionings of investment and empire—we explore dominant notions of empire/colony as key to the work of modernist studies. Given that "modernity" is predicated upon discourses of primitivism, a consideration of the postcolonial Caribbean—as a region that, for better or worse, has come to be identified with notions of hybridity and creolization—is a useful starting point for thinking about race and new modernism. The chapter also provides an entrée into thinking about the Caribbean as a contested site onto which various modernist social actors imposed their own interests. The region is central for figures like Marcus Garvey, William Faulkner, Margaret Mitchell, and Zora Neale Hurston, just to name a few. The Caribbean also became a contested space during the Spanish-American War for various American priorities that would later animate it. The emphasis on *créolité* advanced by Martinican writer and critic Édouard Glissant is useful here, as he drew connections between the Caribbean and the American South (as well as Latin America). His influence in postcolonial and post-structuralist thinking in relation to modernism is evident, for example, in his work on William Faulkner, *Faulkner, Mississippi* (1996). Scholarly work on the Caribbean (such as the 2007 collection *Just Below South: Intercultural Performance in the Caribbean and the U. S. South*) continues to romanticize the region by identifying hybridity as the feature that distinguishes it. We will consider the possibilities and shortcomings of this line of thinking, tracing such discourse back to nineteenth-century Britain—a very different context in certain ways, of course, but one that shares with contemporary postcolonial scholarship a view of Caribbean distinctiveness.

While examining the Caribbean as a primary case study, this chapter will also briefly reference other sites of nationalist contestation—indigenous populations, as well as postcolonial sites such as India, Ireland, and South Africa—to give a sense of the scope of the dynamics that attended a proliferating fragmentation of empire in relation to the rise of modernist performances and ideologies. With that in mind, we will also explore discourses of race and modernism in relation to Cuba, as the island was uniquely situated during the early part of the twentieth century as a stage on which notions of ethnicity and nationality were performed. Cuba was also the site of an emerging dialectic of modernism and primitivism. "Cuba" has long existed as a figuration through which Americans and Europeans have fashioned cultural desire in ambivalent ways. This was particularly true during the height of the philosophical, literary, and artistic context that came to be known as modernism. On one hand, Cuba was a contested space in relation to issues of empire and primitivism. On the other, it was a site of inspiration for artists as varied as Ernest Hemingway, Walker Evans, and Carleton Beals. Consequently, as "Cuba" became increasingly utilized as a rhetorical framework for discussing themes of nation and identity, modernist formulations of race were manufactured through that same framework. When approached through the context of Cuba, modernist discourses of race and identity have striking implications for contemporary scholarly approaches to the geo-social category now called the Global South.

We also see generative comparisons that might be drawn between the modernist figures above from their respective genres of fiction, photography, and journalism. The various ways in which such themes and discourses were identified—and what those identifications signify about the transience of concepts like race and modernism—is what we intend to engage.

Chapter 3 turns from the region of the Global South to the American South, a site that figured prominently in early iterations of modernism. We are especially interested in how formations of race helped authors articulate core southern tropes, such as tradition, individualism, and borders in what we now call the "Southern Renaissance." We end the chapter by focusing on the historical/literary/cultural significances of the notion of "rebirth," itself, as well as the region's preoccupations, major figures, modernist ethos, visual arts, aesthetics, and anxiety over identity. Broader themes emerge here in relation to regionalism, dialect, racial uplift, and urban and rural spaces. Additionally, scholars in southern studies (Leigh Anne Duck, Peter Schmidt, John T. Matthews, Jon Smith, and Deborah Cohn, just to name a few) have brought critical analyses of the South into hemispheric and transnational orbits with discussions of the Global South.

Chapter 4 examines the familiar subject of the Harlem Renaissance's importance in the understanding and evolution of modernism. Significant scholarly attention has been paid to such connections, bringing them into a transatlantic context as well. Some examples include Frank Andre Guridy's *Forging Diaspora* (2010), which foregrounds the significance of Afro-Cuban connections with African American political projects; Philip Curtin's *The Rise and Fall of the Plantation Complex* (1990), which provides an analysis of plantation economies in a global context; and James Smethurst's and George Handley's discussions of post-slavery and post-Reconstruction racial identifications and performances. We will disturb the notion that the Harlem Renaissance was an "event" bound up in a simple historical moment and instead offer its value to modernist studies as a heuristic through which white authors found value in race and racial representation as modes of cultural capital. We end this chapter by thinking through what the South heuristically presents to and performs for a scholar of modernism and race.

In our final chapter, we turn attention to the additional work that has been done at the intersection of race and modernism in specific relation to marketing and consuming performances of racial difference. The waning popularity minstrel shows gave way in the early twentieth century to vaudeville, though the performances of racial stereotypes would continue to play out literally on stage. Starting from the critical distinction between the theoretical terms "performance" and "performativity," we discuss the modernist selling, consuming, and marketing bodies of color. These systems of economic exchange traded on white obsession with "primitivism"; however, they also served as sites for subversive political responses to white supremacy. We will examine some of the shapes those responses took. When taken together with the phenomenon of jazz and its transatlantic significance, these case studies illuminate the important distinction between performance and performativity, which gained analytical traction as new modernism was inaugurated as its own scholarly transition. Methods and strategies for marketing and consuming racial otherness were crucial components of modernist projects. With that in mind, this chapter addresses the politics and economics of modernist ideologies.

And, finally, our project ends with a coda in which we think about identifications of race and modernism as they gesture toward the contemporary sociocultural moment. In focusing on "new modernisms," we will look to the ways in which these identifications have been construed and operationalized after the post-structuralist turn. Without a stable or knowable "history" or "identity" on which to rely, how have scholars made sense of social constructionism in relation to the high-stakes contexts of racialized violence, for example? In what ways have notions of race as a biological marker continued to proliferate in contemporary media and academic outlets? How can we answer the preceding question without falling into the binary of theory and praxis, ideation and experience? What kinds of value—heuristic or otherwise—do signifiers like "blackness" and "modernity" continue to hold, and for whom? In what ways do these contemporary moments rely upon some of the same questions and debates emphasized in the modernist era? How have modernist figures like James Baldwin reemerged both in scholarly and in popular discussions of race, identity, and nation, and what are the possibilities and limitations for such reemergence in new and different contexts (e.g., the quick comparisons that have been made between Baldwin and Ta-Nehisi Coates, as well as references to Baldwin in relation to the Black Lives Matter movement)? We will apply the social theory and discourse analysis that characterize this book to more contemporary modes of political activism regarding race and the nation-state. Our aim in this volume is not to be exhaustive but rather to introduce the careful reader to the problems and possibilities opened by exploring "modern" aesthetics and ethos through episodic visits to regions and historical moments in which both terms reflexively worked together to describe a movement we still conflate with the arc of the twentieth century itself: modernism.

Notes

1 Of note is Nathan Irvin Huggins's earlier work *Harlem Renaissance* (1971), which was a significant but relatively solitary contribution in the field. In contradistinction to the works of Baker and Gates in the subsequent decade, Huggins regarded the Harlem Renaissance as a product of provincialism and political inefficacy in the service of white interests.

2 See Aaron Jaffe, "Who's Afraid of the Inhuman Woolf?" *Modernism/ Modernity*. 23.3 (2016): 491–513.

1

Lost Languages: Expatriate Primitivism and European Modernity in Translation

In 1906, Pablo Picasso presented his friend and source of artistic inspiration, Gertrude Stein, with a portrait of her that he had painted. In a break from the aesthetic of previous portraits of women, Picasso painted Stein not in a provocative and sensual pose but rather seated in intense contemplation, a pose more suited to the intellectual weight of the woman he portrayed. More importantly, his representation of Stein's face cast it as almost set in stone, a hulking and sharply defined mask that hearkened back to African and Iberian masks of femininity. For Picasso, the African mask represented a kind of "lost" aesthetic that had been replaced by the "progress" of civilization; by reconfiguring the work of African and Iberian artists, Picasso aimed to frame his aesthetic as a part of a would-be reclamation of what he suggested had been lost from so-called primitive cultures.

When Stein reciprocated her friend's present seventeen years later, she provided her own portrait of the artist that drew on the same kind of primitivism that Picasso found so compelling in African art. The 1923 poem "If I Told Him: A Completed Portrait of Picasso," is a classic example of Stein's modernist aesthetic. In it, she uses the repetition of words and rhythms to offer an answer to Picasso's imaginative reconfiguration of the African drumbeat, setting a tonal rhythm carried throughout the piece:

> If I told him would he like it. Would he like it if I told him.
>
> Would he like it would Napoleon would Napoleon would would he like it.
>
> If Napoleon if I told him if I told him if Napoleon. Would he like it if I told him if I told him if Napoleon. Would he like it if Napoleon if Napoleon if I told him. If I told him if Napoleon if Napoleon if I told him. If I told him would he like it would he like it if I told him.

Here, in her repletion of monosyllabic words that have equal emphasis, Stein translates the beats of a drum into lyrical poetry. The trisyllabic word "Napoleon" interrupts the beat-beat-beat of the single-syllable words that come before it but also creates its own kind of internal rhyme, for example, with "Napoleon" and "told him." The effect of the poem not only replicates the consistency of the African drumbeat but also alludes to its deviation from and return to a singular rhythm. Stein's influential borrowing from African instruments to create a modern aesthetic cannot be overstated: In the early twentieth century, there was no author more associated with the expatriate movement than Gertrude Stein, and her exchange of portraits with Picasso highlights the ways in which modern artists saw their projects as a reclamation and recreation of "lost" identities. The theme of loss itself was an important rhetorical marker for American expatriates who had migrated to Europe at the turn of the century. Stein called the artists emigrating from America to Europe "une génération perdue," a lost generation. In his *A Moveable Feast*, expatriate author Ernest Hemingway recalled Stein's comments about him and his writing: "'That's what you are. That's what you all are,' Miss Stein said. 'All of you young people who served in the war. You are a lost generation . . . .You have no respect for anything. You drink yourselves to death'" (34–35). In framing the "lost generation's" existential crisis as one of reclaiming what had been lost, Stein offered the solution of literary cubism based on an aesthetic of African culture; the appeal of turning to a non-Western cultural ethos for inspiration suggested to audiences and readers that modernism would reframe the value of art. The exchange of gifts between Picasso and Stein nicely demonstrates how expatriates identified race as a crucial integer to the evolution of modernism in Europe.

Histories of modernism tend to privilege Anglophone traditions, and thus they often emphasize European creative evolutions in arenas like music, art, and literature, and the resulting effects on a burgeoning aesthetic in the US scholarly conflations of a European model of modernism with the particular figure of the American expatriate or immigrant are so entrenched that the story frequently told before the new modernist turn relayed a tale of heroic passages by American writers and artists to sites like London and Paris.

As critic Alfred Kazin notes in his book *On Native Grounds: An Interpretation of Modern American Prose Literature* (1942), major figures of American modernism like Ernest Hemingway, Gertrude Stein, and F. Scott Fitzgerald became synonymous with the "birth" of the literary movement in their post–First World War flight from America to Europe. A constructive discussion of "modernism," then, involves an examination of the origin narratives on which the concept has traditionally relied and the paradigms of expatriation and an imagined Europe that have attended them.

The American expatriate was not, of course, a monolithic figure with a singular vision; however, the historical exodus of people out of America at the turn of the century became one of the more obvious features in tracing a history of modernism. Barbara Will describes expatriate exemplars as those who found their escape from "America [and] its emphasis on material production and consumption" as a way to exercise their "imagination and creativity" (110). The binary of America/Europe operationalized an idea of, on one hand, America's singularity and conventional moralities and modes of art and, on the other hand, a European model of plurality and experimentation specifically centered around Western Europe in the 1920s. An exoticized fantasy of the continent suggested that only in Europe could the American intellectual and artist truly be able to grow and blossom under the auspices of a new dynamic of art-making. American intellectuals flocked to major European centers, which, in turn, established new hierarchies of mentorship among existing cohorts. More important, the dynamics of different artists from various backgrounds and nations interacting together fostered the very sense of plurality and diversity modernist artists came to celebrate in their works. Some of the most foundational literary examples of modernism deal with the notions of expatriation, "American imagination" and European art, and the gaps between the two worlds, for example, works like Hemingway's *The Sun Also Rises* (1926), James's *Daisy Miller* (1879), and Stein's *The Making of Americans* (1925). Indeed, the quintessential modernist hero remains the lone figure of the American expatriate who, in his configuration as a male-in-crisis, repudiates the values and aesthetic of his nation and finds his existential and intellectual home in the vast terrain of a shifting European ethos.

In the precarious scholarly quest to trace the beginning of a modernist aesthetic, though, critical obsession with the origin of the movement's relationship to expatriation necessarily invites us to think about those writers' and artists' interests in race as a way of organizing their social worlds. To be sure, identifications of race were central components in American and European projects long before the turn of the twentieth century. Early twentieth-century American expatriate fashionings of Europe presented "race" (especially notions of blackness) as a tool for complicating and animating artistic endeavors. If cities like Baltimore (for Stein) or Chicago (for Wright) offered only conventional modalities for examining binaries of black/white, their European counterparts in Paris and London offered new avenues for exploring alternate possibilities through which race might open artistic avenues of exploration. The prominence of exchange among many races, ethnicities, and cultural identities was a hallmark of Western Europe in the early twentieth century; the promise of the artistic value presumed to reside inherently in racial otherness drew many Americans' attention to Europe and led in no small part to their development as modern artists.

Modernism centered on play and (re)creation, and race became a crucial part of the modernist explosion of experimentation/play. As figures already interested in the dynamics of cultural exchange—having moved themselves from one societal context to another—expatriate modernist artists found in race a way to expand conventional avenues for their work. Because experimentation with form, voice, affect, experience, language, narrative, and character became central to modernist aesthetics, racial play—that is, variations and improvisations on a theme of racial otherness—operated as a central and foundational part of modernism. Just as Stein used the rhythm of the African drum in her portrait of Picasso, racial vernaculars would become central to expatriate modernist artists' ideas about alienation, exile, fragment, and language itself.

But before exploring the story of how race became (and, indeed, had always been) central to early modernist artists' conceptions of their art, we want to raise the following guiding questions.

Critical queries

Why is modernism often considered to have originated from a fundamentally deracinated (or white) perspective when its early central figures seemed so consumed with imagining race as a resource for their primary aesthetic concerns?

The critical praxis surrounding early modernist studies was anxiously crafting a canon that actively denied space to voices on the margins—women, people of color, and postcolonial writers and artists. Moreover, mid-century scholars of modernism firmly situated the sites of the movement in specific places—London, Paris, Harlem, and Amsterdam—that excluded non-Western and non-Eurocentric spaces and cultures from discussions surrounding a modernist agenda. When issues of race were raised in early critical discussions, the discourse surrounding them often had little to do with identity and agency and focused instead on the formal and aesthetic apparatuses that conceptions of racial otherness offered the (mostly white) writers and artists who made up the first canon of the field. In this chapter, we examine the development and consequences of this discursive focus. We further seek to press the stakes and implications of modernist definitions of race that would see "it" as something of a stable entity that can be described and represented.

How is the figure of the expatriate foundational to the origin narratives about modernism?

Though we should always remain suspicious of origin stories— especially for concepts as broad and complicated as "modernism"— thinking through *why* we consider the expatriate figure as a satisfying opening offers some important guiding questions and queries in complicating a conversation about modernism in our research and our classrooms. Moreover, fixation on race and racial (mis)representation seems to be fundamental to the very figure of the expatriate archetype we explore. Yet, frequently, these canonical writers are posited as being disinvested in race, beyond, perhaps, a superficial fascination with blackness. As the bulk of this chapter shows, however, modern authors of the early twentieth century were not just interested in black/white dynamics in America but central in creative configurations of different nations, people, cultures, societies, and races. As a movement, modernism was fueled by a series of conversations surrounding the opportunities offered by experimentation with form and structure through identifications of race, and with no figure was that experimentation more compelling, more foundational to the ethos of their work, than with the expatriate.

What formalist techniques animated expatriate modernist agendas, and how did those structures both enable a dominant conversation about experimentation and, simultaneously, elide the work of nonwhite authors and artists?

Following this section, and in each chapter, we present a series of "critical concepts" in bold that help to plot a trajectory for the argument that follows. For this chapter, we are especially interested in mapping out terms that allow our readers to follow critical formalist ideas that modernist artists employed to facilitate hybrid modes of aesthetic experimentation; expatriate work frequently married the traditions of both a Western and a non-Western culture in order to play with the gaps between models of articulation and aesthetics. Far from a singular concept or one guided by a sole paradigm of study, multiple configurations of race by expatriate and early modernist artists created a multivocal and elaborate story. We will discuss how those (structural or formalist) ideas helped to craft the rhetoric of modernism that we study today, and we will also explore how those ideas denied entry into modernist cohorts for those artists of color.

What were the political ramifications of modernist experimentation with race in the early decades of the twentieth century?

Many of the early modernist texts shared a romantic ideal of migration and expatriation; thus, modernism's early works often investigate conceptions of an individual's relationship to nationality and capitalist endeavors. Because the very notion of the "modern" frequently gets yoked together with narratives of democracy and emancipation, modernism and progressivism are presumed synonymous in that they supposedly describe upwardly moving trajectories in both literary and political realms. However, as Urmila Seshagiri notes, the very "emancipatory ideals of modernism," such as "the sovereignty of the nation-state, the authority of natural science, the dominance of a free-market economy . . . became charged signifiers for atomizing, dehumanizing processes that would eventually fragment and alienate the very culture they promised to perfect" (10). Indeed, these foundational principles of modernism served as an engine for many exploitative and violent policies among nation-states. Occasionally, modernist scholars seek to articulate an ahistorical model of modernism that, in favor of aesthetic concerns, elides structural dynamics and politics present in artistic representation. Thus, we will discuss some ways in which race in the early twentieth century offered modernist authors opportunities to work through aesthetic concerns, but we are also invested in thinking through the implications of aesthetic choices in relation to the contemporaneous rise of dictatorships, nationalist discourse, racial segregations, and the Holocaust.

By answering these questions and offering some new ones, we hope to expand scholarly discussions about expatriate perspectives on race such that they include a more thorough consideration of how modernism evolved from a movement conceived as deracinated to one that was consumed by anxiety over/for/about race and racial representation. An examination of some key terms/tropes that help tell that story is a productive place to begin. Recalling Stein and Picasso's exchange, our terms are all centered around the notion of language and loss. We begin with the concept of **dialect**, a specific way of speaking that becomes central to the expatriate artist's conception of a new movement. Our interest in language leads to our second concept of **translation**, a term that asks us to think through issues of nation, culture, and exchange. And, finally, we end where we begin—with the expatriate author's use of **primitivism** as the key concept of "loss" and, ironically, the crucial integer in evolving a new ethos of modernism.

Dialect

In attempting to reciprocate the gift of Picasso's portrait, Stein turned to her own artistic tool: language. By careful repetition of certain words, Stein called attention to the power of cadence and rhythm, connecting to the same aesthetic of African art. "If I Told Him" becomes a poem in which Stein channels a different kind of vernacular and attempts to mirror a way of speaking that is decidedly breaking from the traditions of European or American poetry. Her portrait of Picasso, in many ways, positions a modernist agenda inside an African artistic form, and this mode of writing would be foundational to other expatriate authors who found artistic inspiration in her work.

In *The Dialect of Modernism*, Michael North argues that, far from being a corollaries to the work of expatriate modernist writers, race and racial awareness were intimately bound up with the work of modernism from its first iterations. North especially finds expatriate white writers' interests in black voices to be key to the development of modernism: "Three of the accepted landmarks of literary modernism in English," he argues, "depend on racial ventriloquism . . . linguistic mimicry and racial masquerade." North concludes that the reliance on these structures of racial play is central to the evolution of modernism; indeed, they are "strategies without which modernism could not have arisen" (i).

North's argument about the influence of racial awareness and its distribution by white modernist authors feels like a good starting point from which to explore the complex relationship race has to what we understand now as modernist aesthetics. In a part of his book he labels "The Dialect of the Expatriate," North makes a case for the fundamental shift that modernism announces as stemming primarily from the experimentation of the expatriate authors in Europe as they began to play with representations of race in literary and visual art. Noting that Michael H. Levenson offers a somewhat conventional origin to the modernist genealogy with Conrad's *The Nigger of the "Narcissus"* (1897), North asserts that the novel explores new expressive forms largely through the (speculative) question of how one imagines race: thus the work becomes, in his words, "prophetic of a modernism increasingly obsessed with and finally taken over by its black subjects" (37). Shortly after Conrad's book becomes popular, North notes, "European artists were attracted en masse to an African art they knew virtually nothing about and were mesmerized by the way that African masks and statues dislocated all conventional artistic strategies" (59). The attraction to the unfamiliar aesthetics of African art can be seen in the work of visual artists such as Pablo Picasso and literary artists, such as Gertrude Stein, whose friendship and partnership shares an origin story with another "myth" about the beginning of modernism: in the moment that Matisse exposes them both to an African statue he had recently bought at a local store.

As mentioned at the opening of this chapter, Stein and Picasso found a receptacle for their emphases on alienation and exile, both geographically and existentially. As the very font of white alienation, then, expatriate American artists found in Africa (and its corollaries of African diasporic identity) a model for their own aesthetic, a mirror to reflect their experience: "The avant-garde rejects European society, and thus enjoys the freedom of living outside the law, while simultaneously savoring connection to something more authentic found in Africa" (North 67). However, these investments in experimentation and avant-garde aesthetics nonetheless trafficked in rhetorics of authenticity. Innovation and a presumed purer cultural state were co-constitutive appeals. For expatriate writers, the continent of Africa became both a lens to see through and a mask to wear. Many of the figures we come to think of as representative of conventional modernism—T. S. Eliot, Ezra Pound, Wallace Stevens, Claude McKay, and William Carlos Williams, to name a few—worked through their understandings of a modernist agenda via racial masquerade surrounding the mystery and allure of an African mask (both literal and figurative). Stein's influence, of course, dominates so much of expatriate culture, her declaration of the "lost generation" still operating as a metonym for contemporary understandings of a cohort of the early modernist authors. This obsession with "representing" race resulted in the production of ideologically loaded renderings of racial otherness that inevitably reflected the interests of the artists who made them.

The binary of an Anglocentric-European modernism in which dialect was in vogue—celebrated as "authentic" and more valuable—and an African American (or even African diasporic) tradition in which it was a confining reminder of oppression hardly gets articulated by scholars beyond North and Baker prior to the 1990s. "For this reason," North sums up in his introduction, "it is impossible to understand either modernism without reference to the other, without reference to the language they so uncomfortably shared, and to the political and cultural forces that were constricting that language at the very moment modern writers of both races were attempting in dramatically different ways to free it" (11). Borrowing from Henry Louis Gates, Jr., North reframes the dialect of modernism used by expatriate writers like Pound and Stein not as "mere deviation or deformation, but a particular *use* of language" (72). However, the bifurcation of dialect as a mimicry of speech (through colloquial or local color translations of, for example, African Americans) and as a tool used to critique language itself is tremendously important in teasing out what the stakes were for modernist writers of color and their (largely white) expatriate colleagues.

Dialect as a kind of verbal mask ultimately proved to be one of the defining features of expatriate modernist writing as well as one of its most divisive. Experimentation with the perceived limits of language remains a hallmark of what continues to be considered prototypical modernist technique. However, such technique also has a troubling and complicated history of masking, racial play, and the willful naiveté of white expatriate authors who saw in race a conduit for a vernacular of disenfranchisement they sought to employ. Thus, it is painfully fraught, especially considering its ramifications in relation to exile, the state, and nationhood.

Translation

When Picasso presented his portrait of Gertrude Stein in 1906, Stein naturally wanted to reciprocate her friend's gift. However, Stein was unskilled in the medium in which Picasso worked. Instead of taking up paint to try her hand at representing the artist, Stein, instead, picked up her pen. Her portrait of Picasso showcases Stein's attempt to answer her friend's mastery of the visual form with her own mastery of the literary one. To create her own work of art, Stein had to adapt the visual form to her burgeoning aesthetic of poetry by reinventing both the idea of form and the tradition of poetics. Fundamental to her adaptation was a sense of play, of mimicry, and connecting two disparate elements of artistic endeavor. We might consider Stein's work, then, as a kind of translation, not of just the visual to the literary, but of the form to the subject, a translation of an idea to an artistic object. The idea of translation itself becomes a central heuristic for thinking through the difficult work of representing race through an artistic lens, and it invites us to work through the complicated idea of nationhood itself, a central anxiety of those whom we now think of as expatriates. Key to the foundation of expatriation was voluntary exile from countries of origin, a rejection of nationalism and national identity and an adherence to a presumably global perspective. How race becomes central to that identity is a multifaceted narrative— race not only offered a means for experimentation for artists who migrated physically and intellectually away from their home nations but also operated as a symbol for the very act of migration itself. Early expatriate writers experimenting with modernism might "adopt" different cultural and racial attributes as part of their fantasies of migration; rootless in their aesthetic, they could find ostensible roots in other races and cultures. In this way, they still appealed to authenticity despite the nominal rejection of traditional norms.

If "African American dialect" offered expatriate authors a way to speak in a different voice and craft their own vernacular, other nations and cultures offered a wandering mind the chance to think differently about broad concepts like time, religion, and language itself. And yet, "if we want to think of modernism globally, we must face the fact that," as Eric Hayot notes, "any attempt to get past the Eurocentric story about what modernism is and does must encounter, first, the history of that Eurocentric story as it has been incorporated into national systems of literature" (152).

If we broaden the lens beyond the continent of Africa and beyond the reductive binary of black/white, we can locate "race" at the intersection of much of what we think of as the origins of a modernist aesthetic. Pericles Lewis, for example, makes much of Joyce's ending to *A Portrait of the Artist as a Young Man* (1916) and Stephen Dedalus's determination "to forge in the smithy of my soul the uncreated conscience of my race," a statement that Lewis finds rooted in the very foundations of the birth of the modern novel. For Joyce, "the racial conscience is a sort of god that Stephen plans to serve through his writing" which, in turn, revises the "literary archetype of nineteenth-century realism, the novel of disillusionment. The heroic narrator-protagonist became, in Joyce's vision, the focus for re-awakening of national consciousness centered on the awareness that individuals are both subjects and objects of historical processes" (*Modernism, Nationalism, and the Novel 2*). Taking another example, Helen Carr asserts that Ezra Pound's obsession with fragmentation of form—long considered one of the hallmarks of modernist aesthetics—can be traced back to his obsession with the "supreme version of this in the superimpositions of the Chinese ideogram, from which he drew, as he put it, 'a whole basis of aesthetic' . . . the collages of modernism came out of a hybrid, multiracial world" (87).

In his book *Ideographic Modernism* (2010), Christopher Bush notes, however, that modernism's co-opting of the ideograph/ideogram was not, in any way, rooted in a profound desire to replicate Chinese writing in some "authentic" way, but was instead a stark translation, "Chinese writing as imagined in the West" (xvi). Some of the first modern artists became interested in other nations and cultural texts not to reproduce them faithfully or to say something "true" about the culture itself but to find in exoticism a form for experimentation and hybridity—two features of modernist aesthetics that define the movement as people have come to know it. In modernist configurations, then, Africa, China, or India ceases to be a discourse or a lens and instead becomes, in Bush's phrasing, a "myth": "not primarily in the sense that it is false, but rather . . . as a topos for demonstrating a commitment to *form*" (73). Modernists' emphases on the formal structures that underpin artistic endeavors take precedence over any kind of fidelity to the subjects or cultural products being represented. Under the auspices of a kind of play or what we might think of as experimentation, the form became central to the undertaking, and race offers a chance for hybridity that Western artists felt useful to their tasks.

The idea of translation becomes a useful one in complicating attempts by modernist artists to present their work as a kind of pastiche for racial/regional otherness, when they wrote primarily in English and came predominantly from Anglophone contexts. In thinking through such notions of translations, though, we also must consider the complications arising from identifications with nations and nationalities. Questions about reading and translating proliferate in modernist codifications of discourse or texts not their own. Brent Hayes Edwards suggests that, in thinking of the term "African diaspora," for example, we must start with the truth that "the cultures of black internationalism can only be seen *in translation*" (7; emphasis in original). Embedded within the project of investigating modernist imaginations of race, then, we must "approach such a project . . . by attending to the ways that discourses of internationalism *travel*, the ways they are translated, disseminated, reformulated, and debated in transnational contexts marked by difference" (7).

As a poet, Pound considered himself a "translator" of many foreign texts, and the role of "translation" itself became a trope for the poet's role within imagism as a formalist movement. And yet, as Rebecca Beasley notes in her "Modernism's Translations," Pound was not attempting to translate the texts he encountered verbatim for his readers but instead to compose "deliberately opaque texts, which draw the reader's attention to the translator's linguistic and metrical choices" (558). Such a process "constructs a productive foreignness in the translation by mixing discourses across periods and cultures"

(558). Though useful in refashioning the original work outside of its cultural context, Pound's defamiliarization in his translations obscures its source material by, in Beasley's words, "rewriting the source text to serve modernist cultural agendas" (558). Not unlike the concept of imitation that, as mentioned above, shows the original it approximates to be its own illusion, defamiliarization can be troubling and also offer possibilities for thinking productively about the ways in which familiarity could never be a possible outcome in the first place.

If modernist expatriates founded their senses of identity on forced migrations away from their erstwhile national identities, that move was brokered by an ambivalence or anxiety over their connection (or the lack thereof) to a concept of a "state." To be an expatriate, then, might also mean to be considered of a different race, a rootless wanderer without a state. The concept of "national identity" becomes central to any conceptions of how race might operate for expatriates. National identity also necessarily involves racial identity since, as Patricia E. Chu argues in *Race, Nationalism, and the State in British and American Modernism* (2006), it is the state itself that had a role "in creating and sustaining administrable identities and subjectivities" that cross lines of gender, class, and race (14). Far from providing a way to coalesce around a stable center, translations and configurations of nation-states reveal that stable center to be a myth suiting the interests of those perpetuating it. To put it differently, it is translations all the way down.

Any project seeking to chart a connection between modernism(s) and race must always have in its foreground a functioning idea of how "race" matters in connection with nation. The social stakes of this classificatory effort have always been high, of course, and the decades when modernist sensibilities were at their peak were no exception. Definitions of "race" vis-à-vis "nation" took center stage in the Jim Crow laws that governed a white supremacist social order in the American South, while fascism gathered wind in its sails across Europe. David Ayers reminds us that "the role of 'race' in the modernism of the 1920s and 1930s should be mapped, therefore, in terms of the primacy of the universalism which already sought to govern . . . the ambiguously situated category of nation" (159). When we look at the work of writers like Pound and Eliot, we encounter modernist authors—whether expatriates or no—whose ideas about race were forged by the dynamics surrounding their relationships to a projected "national identity" (by way of claim or disavowal).

Modernist scholars of both Eliot and Pound, though, have to contend with the authors' views on race and representation because the consequences of some of these views directly connect with the genocide of events like the Holocaust, "a transnational event," as Phyllis Lassner notes, "that in its specifically defined temporal, ideological and experimental extremes adds crucial critical facets to debates about race and modern culture" (193). The temptation to disassociate the rise of nationalism and the literary movement of modernism is an important one to avoid, as it effectively eradicates the participation of modern expatriate authors in perpetuating particular ideas about race that had devastating consequences in their own time. Lassner claims, if we want to embrace the flurry of art and writing that has been "tacked on to extend the timeline of modernism" in the 1940s, we must also take serious stock of the rhetoric that modernist expatriate artists used that could be co-opted for fascism, nativism, and ultranationalism.

Primitivism

When Picasso imagined an aesthetic that would recreate his portrait of Stein, he did not look to innovations in reproduction or ways in which he might use techniques to make his subject appear more concrete. He, instead, turned to the African mask as his inspiration for Stein's figure. In turn, Stein's adoption of the rhythms of African dance and dialect marked an aesthetic by which modern expatriate artists sought to reclaim a "lost culture." In a similar way that "dialect" came to be used as a tool with which white modernist expatriate authors could experiment with language on a more rudimentary level, the turn toward the "primitive" by expatriates (especially in relation to visual art) remains one of the key terms in an exploration of how race functioned in early modernist contexts. In his recent and perceptive study *Literary Primitivism* (2017), Ben Etherington notes that the very notion of the primitive "was an aesthetic project formed in reaction to the zenith of imperialist expansion at the start of the twentieth century" (xi). Imperialist endeavors that sought, on the one hand, to colonize or integrate so-called "primitive spaces" simultaneously fixated on the cultural debris left in the wakes of their enterprises. Thus, modernist aesthetics were invested in "rekindl[ing] the primitive by means of their art. As such, primitivism was a project specific to this world-historical situation: an undertaking to become primitive in a world where, it seemed, such a possibility had been voided" (xi).

What the concept of race offered expatriate modernist artists was something of an interlocutor identity, a means of transport from the cosmopolitan intellectual to the barbarous and savage; it was a mask of a different sort, not necessarily linguistic but visceral and stark. One of the most-well-documented examples of modernist consumption of the primitive is Picasso's obsession with African art. Early in his career, Picasso was drawn to African indigenous art and to what he saw as its potential for mystery. As someone removed from the social or cultural world of the continent, Picasso immersed himself in the fetish with little regard for its production or context. As Gikandi notes, "The fact that Picasso had an intimate relationship with African objects is not in doubt; but there is little evidence of an interest in Africans as human beings and producers of culture beyond his general interest and involvement in anti-colonial and other radical movements" (33). Picasso's fixation on Africa was part of a larger movement, sometimes called *négrophilie*, defined by Sweeney as "a modernist primitivism, brimming with the dynamic and vigorous energies and contradictions of all the various strands of modernisms" (4). *Négrophilie* reimagined blackness not as a site of the "base, backwards, and lacking any cultural presence," but instead a world of "exotic legitimacy," where modern artists could experiment with form, structure, content, aesthetic, and style by borrowing the cultural primitive as their muse (4). Picasso, of course, was not the only artist who looked to other continents for inspiration: the French impressionist Paul Gauguin famously fetishized the landscapes and inhabitants of French colonial islands Martinique and Tahiti. Though he stayed on the island only for a brief period of time, the works he created were among his most famous, and Martinique and its people continued to inspire him throughout his life.

While white, modern artists explored their obsession with blackness by experimenting (a basic definition of *négrophilie*), the more complicated notion of *négritude* involves a more thorough exploration of subject-object in relation to race and primitivism. Etherington defines *négritude* as a "cultural movement of the black francophone middle class, which saw itself from two irreconcilable perspectives—as the civilized subject and barbarous object of European civilization—and which resolved to negate that civilization by giving itself over to its objectification as 'Negro'" (vx). Just as "dialect" bifurcated white and African American modernist aesthetics, so, too did *négritude* establish the border. On the one hand, there is a kind of discourse of play where the expatriate artists can imagine the possibilities of the primitive despite their place at the top of the imperialist enterprise. On the other hand, with *négritude* the artists find the gaps between how they view themselves and how they *are* viewed.

Underneath many of these early examples of modern explorations of form, one finds that the expatriate fixation on race does not fundamentally focus on "blackness" per se. Beyond *négritude* and *négrophilie*, modernism's early artistic articulations of primitivism employ a broader definition of race. Carr notes that it is in the cultural translation of these racial forms that modernist expatriate writers found "elemental, pared down, limpidly intense poetry . . . [a] turn away from Western modernity to the distant and archaic, the Japanese, the Chinese, the early Greek, or the ancient Hebrew" (64). Such a play between poles of primitive/modern might seem obvious for a movement labeled "modernism," but it is useful to note that the appeal of primitivism seemed to define modernist projects almost from the beginnings of what we have come to understand as the nascent stages of modernism itself.

Race as a concept operated as a way in which the first modernist writers could approach both structures and aesthetics alien to them and use the techniques of racial representation and identification in their work. Because modernist figures deployed racialized tropes with little engagement with their effects, the history of the movement is rife with the production and perpetuation of racial stereotypes. It is not surprising that many of the canonized authors we refer to as conventional modernists had difficult relationships with race, both as a literary idea and as a political one. With writers like Pound and Eliot frequently excoriated for their virulent anti-Semitism, and many early modernist artists caught up in the sweep of nationalist dictatorships and the rise of Nazism and totalitarianism, it is easy to see the political implications of engaging with a concept of race primarily as a synonym for primitivism. John Frank Williams's *The Quarantined Culture: Australian Reactions to Modernism, 1913–1939* charts Australia's political reaction to a modernist aesthetic, for example. In it, Williams argues that the nation saw its status as a "modern nation" as being forged by a sinister pluralism with "modern artists," peopled by an "inchoate grouping of racial supremacists, anti-Semites, anti-bolshevists, protectionists, anti-industrialists and the leaders of an elitist and conservative art-world establishment" (5).

Finally, expatriate tropes about race and primitivism were critical tools used to enjoy the simplicity of subject and object apart from any concerns of empire and capitalism. Carl Einstein's "On Primitive Art" (1919), defines the aesthetic as "the rejection of the capitalistic art tradition. European mediateness [*sic*] and tradition must be destroyed; there must be an end to formalist fictions. If we explode the ideology of capitalism, we will find beneath it the sole valuable remnant of this shattered continent, the precondition for everything new, the masses of simple people . . . the artist" (124). Thus part of the work for scholars of "new modernism" is to locate the sites where modernist ideas about the primitive and the avant-garde collapse in on each other, revealing the ways in which the latter relied upon the former. Ruth B. Phillips notes the gap between what modern artists said about the primitive and what they practiced:

> The modernist campaign for the acceptance of African and other primitive arts as fine art turned on a central paradox. It required the replacement of the primary references of the term "primitive" as "backward" and "inferior" with diametrically opposite references to the "advanced" and the "superior." The modernists, in other words, insisted on retaining the core meanings of "primitive" as primal, simple, and natural, converting the negative charges associated with these terms—irrational, pre-industrial, and unsophisticated—, into a set of positive attributes. . . . Equally importantly, the modernists' project of redefinition transformed the "primitive" from an objectified category with fixed meanings into a movement—primitiv-ism—which was processual and open-ended. (6)

In short, modernist projects were aimed at a profit-based primitivism, their utility bound up in the process of making art new again for the cosmopolitan intellectual at the very top of the capitalist hierarchy. However, a crucial difference between the modernist aesthetic and the one practiced at different historical/literary moments was the expatriate authors' conception of race as the central lens through which to experiment with primitive cultures and reify them for intellectual consumption.

Inside imperialist ideological frameworks, "primitive art" was both advocated for and voraciously consumed. Gikandi nicely sums up the consequences of such a move and its persistent rhetoric in discourses on the movement still today: "The practitioners of modernism had themselves started the process of containment . . . the Other needed to be evacuated from the scene of the modern so that it could enter the institutions of high art" (457). In thinking about how early examples of modern artists—especially expatriates who were ultimately concerned with fidelity (or the lack thereof) to political causes and national identifications—used notions of race to advance primitivist projects, one should not lose sight of the imperialist underpinnings of many attempts at "translation."

Thinking outward

As we discuss connections between articulations of modernism and concepts of race, we envision the remaining chapters as a series of visits to various sites at specific historical moments in which racial identification became a key animating force in the evolution and operationalization of modernist ideology. With so many of the early (white) artists of modernism experimenting with what they considered the utility of race to explore aesthetic possibilities, the ongoing colonial enterprises of the late nineteenth and early twentieth centuries remain ever present conceptually. In the chapter that follows, we move from the libraries and salons of European nations in which modernist artists explored the art and culture of the African continent and into a new space entirely: the Caribbean.

In shifting a discussion from Europe to the "Global South" of the Caribbean, we still encounter many of the same problems of perception, authorship, and reception explored in this chapter. However, by moving from a region associated with the birth of canonical modernism and into a politically, artistically, and culturally contested site, new questions and problems arise. Specifically, we will think about imperial projects in relation to racial formation, especially when dovetailing with notions of ownership, colony, revolution, and nationhood. The Caribbean was a nexus of European economic and cultural investments, and writers and artists saw in the region aesthetic possibilities for their own projects. Thinking about the ways in which such investments crafted racial identifications helps us situate our discussion in new modernist analytical modes in a couple of ways. First, we posit race not as ontological signifier but as a sociocultural trope. Second, we reject a wholesale or singular Anglo-European/American association with modernism and instead suggest the necessity of looking to a transatlantic and postcolonial South.

2

The Birth of Many Nations: Imperial Modernisms in the Caribbean

During the height of his popularity, Ernest Hemingway and his wife, the famed novelist Martha Gellhorn, purchased a house just on the outskirts of Havana. The couple nicknamed their new home Finca Vigía, "lookout farm." Though Gellhorn and Hemingway would split just five years later, Hemingway kept his lookout farm in Cuba. The island nation just off the coast of Florida was a source of endless fascination for Hemingway, and he wrote the bulk of two of his most famous novels at Finca Vigía: *For Whom the Bell Tolls* (1940) and the Pulitzer Prize–winning *The Old Man and the Sea* (1952). Cojimar, a tiny port town just a few miles east of Havana, was the inspiration for the setting of the latter. Hemingway's presence in Cuba was just as quotidian as it was literary: he walked the streets with the locals, shopped at local markets, and even arranged playdates with his sons and local children. As relationships between the United States and Cuba began to deteriorate, Hemingway remained loyal to his farm and the Caribbean nation. He felt at home among the people of Cuba and declared himself a native islander. When he won the Nobel Prize in 1954, Hemingway donated the plaque to a local church in El Cobre. There was perhaps no place on Earth that Hemingway, the world traveler and chronicler of the rootless American expatriate, felt more comfortable than Cuba.

Hemingway's love of the Caribbean is not unique among modernist writers. We can easily turn to Zora Neale Hurston's anthropological work in Haiti and Jamaica, for instance, in *Tell My Horse* (1938) as just one example of the kind of work overtly invested in the region. The Caribbean itself was a site of endless inspiration and fascination for European and American modernist writers of the twentieth century. The myriad of cultures, the exchanges (both linguistic and cultural), and the broad and complicated history of the nations that made up the Caribbean were a kind of symbol for the interplay and experimentation of identity that marked a modernist ethos. Reading modernism in concert with the Caribbean is a fairly new phenomenon. When the transnational turn in new modernist studies began almost two decades ago, the field necessarily also began incorporating the work of postcolonial studies and paradigms to investigate the complicated exchanges between imperial projects and colonial subjects. Since that time, scholars have published extensively on multiple sites where colony and empire play formative roles in the birth and evolution of modernism.[1] We will focus our attention in this chapter on how formulations of race have operated in empire-building efforts in the modernist era, specifically as they took shape in the nations that make up the Caribbean.

Debates surrounding the role of the Caribbean in the early twentieth century make the site a particularly fecund one for explorations of how interests in race animated modern artists in the decades from 1900 to 1950. Further, the fact that many of the authors we consider to be canonical and central to the world of modern literature were actively involved in writing about or pondering the question of the Caribbean also makes the space a central one for our project. Since its colonial contact late in the fifteenth century, the Caribbean has been a site dominated by imperialist projects, and its complicated history is replete with anxieties over ownership, power, enslavement, borders, nationhood, and colonial discourses. Starting with the Spanish-American Wars of Independence (1808–33), multiple nations vied for ownership of the islands so as to consolidate empire and mine the region's natural resources.

But by the early twentieth century—at precisely the time that modernist artists began to challenge tradition and authority in their own contexts—the questions of ownership and independence become even more fraught for the region that came to be known as the Caribbean. The emphases on the region and acquisition during the beginnings of modernism can be explained in several ways. First, the discourses surrounding enslavement, a crucial feature of the capitalist enterprise in the Caribbean became a major anxiety for imperial investors who saw in the region a site for enriching their status. Though most of the nations who were involved in ownership and investment in the region abolished slavery between 1811 and 1865, the second half of the nineteenth and early part of the twentieth century brought with them an unsettling economic anxiety over how the Caribbean would function in a modern world. For some nations, like Britain, the model to replace enslavement involved indentured labor, which offered the discourse of independence but practically re-entrenched the plantation model by continuing to refuse workers economic autonomy. With enslaved Africans leaving plantations by the late nineteenth century, British investors turned to cheap labor sources in Asia, and by 1906, many of the indentured laborers working in the British Caribbean were from China, India, and Southeast Asia. In this early twentieth-century Caribbean, the deconstruction of plantation economies led to a new capitalist model that continued to deny workers a place in the enterprise other than that of cheap, unskilled labor.

The Caribbean also became a site of anxiety over the issue of rebellion and revolution in the early twentieth century. Already a fraught space with a difficult history, the Caribbean was known to European and American writers and artists primarily through the wars waged to control it and by the uprisings and revolutions that took place by the enslaved populations brought there. The most well-known example of a people fighting for independence through uprising is the Haitian Revolution that began in 1791. Led by the charismatic figure of Toussaint l'Ouverture, enslaved Haitians fought against several imperialist European forces (including France, Spain, and Britain) to gain their independence, ultimately securing it in 1804. By the dawn of the twentieth century, however, Haiti was a politically unstable nation struggling to face its economic realities (its efforts toward independence left the nation deeply in debt to America, France, and Germany). When the First World War broke out, the United States sent troops to Haiti, only to end up occupying the country for over twenty years. The destabilization of Haiti mirrors that of other nations in the region, and the Caribbean remained a space of contestation and possible conquest for European and American forces.

The Spanish-American War in 1898 also contributed to the region's importance for Europe and America in the early twentieth century. When the USS *Maine* exploded and sank in the harbor of Havana in February of 1898, then-president William McKinley was forced to intervene in a local conflict for Cuba's independence that had been going on for decades. Many Americans, galvanized by propaganda against Spain, backed the war, and some of the artists and writers who became instrumental in the modernist movement either participated in the conflict or staked critical political investment in its outcome.[2] As a result of the economic and imperial interest in Cuba's nationhood, and through the 1898 Treaty of Paris that ended the war, America's global power was further solidified. The United States became the temporary overseer of Cuba, as well as gaining control over the territories of Puerto Rico, Guam, and the Philippines. At the beginning of the twentieth century, American investment (economic, political, and discursive) in the Caribbean was at its zenith.

As the nations of the Caribbean became contested spaces for imperial rule, they also consolidated in modernist texts and art as exotic sites for escapist fantasies. At the start of the twentieth century, the Caribbean became a space for tourism and importation of "exotic" goods. In the United States especially, "banana boats"—quick frigates designed to quickly transport perishable fruit from the Caribbean to the mainland—afforded Americans the opportunity to sample fruits and spices that could not be grown locally. As the availability of these products increased, so, too, did American appetites for them. By the 1920s, British colonies in the Caribbean, especially, became sites for tourists to visit. Popular for their beaches and for the promise of "exotic" cultural hybridity, nations like Jamaica, Barbados, Bahamas, and Antigua were flooded by European tourists keen on experiencing "authentic" island cultures. The islands also became popular subjects for many of the figures we think of as mainstays in modernist literature and art.

Critical queries

Why was the Caribbean such a site of contestation for modern artists? Because many of the authors we know as central to the modern canon were from nations and empires already invested—in many different modes—with the Caribbean through conflict, war, plantation models, importation, and tourism, it makes sense that the region would figure prominently in their work. However, in exploring why the Caribbean became such an important site for modernists, we also discuss in this chapter some reasons why the region was so ripe for those authors who were at pains to "make new" an artistic aesthetic that relied heavily on invention, experimentation, and improvisation. Of course, every nation, language, or cultural site is a hybrid product of multiple forces interacting. But inasmuch as political dominance contributes to the image of a stable nation-state that was never contingent or in question, the Caribbean came to be seen (by modernists and contemporary scholars alike) as synonymous with the notion of hybridity. In this view, it was (and remains for many) a site presumably set apart by virtue of cultures coming together and interacting with one another in complicated ways. This ethos that fashions the Caribbean as unique in its creolization aided modernists in projecting their own aesthetic and ideological endeavors onto the region. Interests in racial and ethnic "otherness," as well as an obsessive ambivalence regarding autonomy and representation, found fertile ground in the Caribbean as a metaphor for multivocality.

In addition, the wholesale importation of enslaved and indentured workers from, among other places, Africa and parts of Asia began to populate the islands. The Caribbean was thus at once a space both safe and exotic—safe because it had been dominated by imperial investments but exotic because its workforce was comprised of a variety of unfamiliar cultures. Additionally, modern artists enjoyed the notion of revolution and independence, and the space became a kind of metonym for the constant work toward liberation. Hemingway, for example, found in Cuba a sense of freedom and play that he did not encounter anywhere else, and Claude McKay posited his home nation of Jamaica as the ultimate site of fight and revolution.

What modes of creativity were possible in the Caribbean after colonial contact?

Because modernists wanted, first and foremost, to narrate a break from previous aesthetic traditions through experimentation of form, structure, character, mode, genre, and narrative, they saw in the Caribbean an easy intermediary between old and new epistemologies. Concepts like hybridity and creolization, attached to the Caribbean as already mentioned, were significant ideas within modernist projects. Having a region like the Caribbean under the nominal authority of a European political system created a resource for modern artists to experiment with form in a setting that was at once familiar and

decidedly exotic. The notion of fragmentation, too, was foundational
to modernists' attempts to grapple with the loss of a shared, communal
ideal. In the islands making up the Caribbean, different cross sections
of cultures and people were brought in to feed a capitalist endeavor
that continued to blossom well after the abolition of slavery by
European nations. The fragmentation of cultures, histories, people,
communities, social actors, and nations in the Caribbean created for
modernists the very font of the fragment trope itself. T. S. Eliot would
write *The Waste Land* about "these fragments I have shored against
my ruins," but for the modern writer, the Caribbean offered those
fragments as a physical manifestation of the poetic ideal.

*What kind of identifications (gender, national, class, and sexual) were
foundational to imperial projects in the Caribbean?*
We have already discussed the history of the Caribbean as being
primarily informed by the bringing together of a multitude of
different nations, races, cultures, and people. An important element
of that analysis is thinking about how imperial enterprises in the
Caribbean operationalized various identifications of class, sexuality,
gender, and race. Clearly, modernist writers were invested in asking
probing questions about "identity," whether as an existential endeavor
or as a more personal project of self-discovery. With the Caribbean
as a backdrop, these questions centered in important ways around
notions of race, the diversity within the region offering modern artists
various points of entry for their work.

Similarly, because so much of the culture of the Caribbean became
synonymous with multiplicity and cultural exchanges, modernists
plotted a revision of conventional European and American ideas

about class, gender, and sexuality. Inasmuch as modern artists were at pains to craft or reimagine subjectivity over and against "stable" modes of being, they relished what they took to be a far more liberating source of variability in the Caribbean. The region became a more permissive site for modernist experimentation that did not rely upon conventionality or a master narrative but instead promoted the exploration of identity as an amalgam of different (often competing) scripts. Modernist writers and artists would embrace this subjective instability as a central feature in presenting a fragmented and, ultimately, incomplete understanding of one's identity in relation to the world. In the critical concepts that follow, we will go into a deeper exploration of how modernist figures attempted to answer the questions above and of what the stakes were in doing so. We will be especially interested in the modernist author's affection for the Caribbean as a site of exchange and **hybridity**, whereby ideas, languages, and cultures connect and intermingle. And just as Hemingway was drawn to the troubled history and political upheaval of Cuba, we will investigate the role that **colonial trauma** had on the modernist imagination of the region. Finally, we present the Caribbean as a kind of **other South** that connected to American ideas on imperial conquest in relation to the American South.

Hybridity

Hemingway's love of the Cuban culture largely hinged on his rich appreciation for its multiple linguistic and cultural exchanges; he found in the Caribbean nation an objective correlative for the kind of interplay with histories and cultures that marked many of his characters' search for identity in his novels. In our "Critical Queries" section above, we asked what a project deemed modernist might find of value in a Caribbean space. In other words, how did the Caribbean site foreground important concepts modernist artists took to be central to their aesthetic? Because our volume in this series is especially interested in how modernist techniques use, imagine, revise, contest, and complicate notions of race, we might more specifically ask: What about the Caribbean offered a particularly fruitful space for modern artists to experiment with new conceptions of race and subjectivity? In the preceding chapter, we discussed how "modernity" is predicated upon discourses of primitivism. Postcolonial framings of the Caribbean as a site characterized by hybridity and creolization serve as a useful entrée into new modernist analyses of race as a central constitutive element in early twentieth-century aesthetics and politics? In her study, *The Caribbean Postcolonial* (2004), Shalini Puri argues,

> The sheer number and nuance of the Caribbean's accounts of hybridity, its diverse sources, modalities, and consequences, are unparalleled in any other region of the world. As an archipelago whose culture was forged in the crucible of colonialism and slavery from what Derek Walcott has called a "shipwreck of fragments," [sic] discourses of hybridity have been central to the Caribbean's political culture. For the Caribbean has had to negotiate its identities in relation to Native America; to Africa and Asia, from where most of its surviving inhabitants came; to Europe, from where its colonizing settlers came; and to the United States of America, its imperial neighbor. (2)

Puri notes that, in the region, there emerged a "poetics of hybridity . . . from Creole poetics, to mulatto aesthetics, to magic and marvelous realism" (2). Indeed, scholarly work on the Caribbean romanticizes the region by identifying hybridity as the key feature that distinguishes its appeal to modernist studies, with examples like the collection *Just Below South: Intercultural Performance in the Caribbean and the U. S. South* (2007) and *The Creolization Reader* (Robin Cohen and Paola Toninato, eds., 2010).

And yet, as Seshagiri rightly points out, the emphasis on hybridity by modernist artists does not mirror the anxieties it produced culturally in imperial political discourse, where "disruptions in the continuity of racial identity—through miscegenation, geographical displacement, religious conversion, or political upheaval . . . engendered scientific as well as cultural anxieties about hybridity, contamination, and degeneration" (8). The trope of hybridity, then, posited the Caribbean as a site of both attraction and repulsion—an ambivalence that modernist authors and artists would use as a cornerstone in their work. Advanced by Martinican writer and critic Édouard Glissant, the idea of *créolité* is useful to think through the gap between modernist emphases on hybridity and the ramifications thereof. According to critic Valérie Loichot, "the process of creolization . . . [represents a] complex cultural, familial, and racial diversity impossible to fix in one static definition" (Munro and Britton 88). Perhaps the most important part of the idea of *créolité* is its emphasis on fluidity, for it is "an unpredictable dynamic process, which leads to openness rather than fixity" (Munro and Britton 88). The concept of *créolité* thus offered much to a modernist enterprise focusing not on stasis but on fluidity and experimentation.

Charles W. Pollard's *New World Modernisms* (2004) argues that the emphasis on creolization also critically connects with the connections between artists engaged in the modernist enterprise. Taking as his example the influence of T. S. Eliot on the Caribbean poets Kamau Brathwaite and Derek Walcott—the former of whom claims Eliot as the "only 'European influence' I can detect and will acknowledge," and the latter of whom claims of the poet, "there is no writer of poetry in English who does not owe him a debt" (qtd. in Pollard 2)—Pollard argues, "While Brathwaite and Walcott come of age as poets at the end of the age of Eliot, they are not overwhelmed or stifled by his reputation . . . they freely and selectively reshape Eliot's modernism— they creolize it—to achieve their own purposes; in the process, they create vibrant and complementary New World modernist poetics" (4). The important part of this poetics of creolization is not in how such a poetics might "homogenize cultures to eliminate ethnic, cultural, national, or ideological conflict" but in how it might instead "recognize the possibility of continuity and discrepancy, interdependence and resistance" (5). As signifiers, then, hybridity and creolization do the work of situating borders—literary, cultural, social, historical, national, and racial—even as they challenge the contiguousness and stability of those same lines. In what V. S. Naipaul calls "new world debris" (33), one finds rhetorical tools that proved fundamental to modernist projects.

Colonial trauma

Havana in the 1940s was a site of upheaval—political and economic revolution affected every aspect of Cuban culture, and Hemingway found in that space and time a vibrancy and immediacy that made his modernist projects about identity relevant and important in a way that other nations and identities didn't allow. Indeed, it is difficult—if not impossible—to disentangle the notion of "modernism" from a history of colonialism and the systematic classifications of race that facilitated imperial projects. History is replete with instances of the very word "modern" doing critical work of bounding and silencing. Among other things, the term was used to justify the forced enslavement of indigenous populations, the gradual depletion and ruination of ecological and cultural spaces, the forced migration of entire populations to work as indentured laborers, and the imposition of a hierarchical rule that privileged an imperialist political structure. Indeed, as Alejandro Mejías-López argues in his book *The Inverted Conquest: The Myth of Modernity and the Transatlantic Onset of Modernism* (2009), the twin ideas of modernity and coloniality are "inseparably linked" (11), but the casual linking of the two descriptors elides in its own right. After all, as Mejías-López suggests, empires would position themselves as the sole arbiters of the very definition of modernism itself. The consequences of imperial framing of modernism are severe: "Although connected at first to aesthetics and philosophy, in the nineteenth century this concept of modernity became associated almost exclusively with (northern) European material, technological, and, to a lesser degree, political changes, understood as the necessary result of 'modern' (i.e. Enlightened) reason" (18).

Thus, one of the priorities for new modernist scholars has been to take substantive account of how notions of empire and colonial enterprise took shape in the modernist era. Also worth emphasizing is how, in the decades following the abolition of slavery by the UK, the empire/colony binary emerged and evolved along with attendant anxieties over how to deal with economic and cultural investments in postcolonial spaces. In their introduction to *Modernism and Empire* (2000), editors Howard J. Booth and Nigel Rigby argue that the most fertile decades for growth and evolution of modern artists were also the ones that saw the pinnacle of British imperial expansion. What's more, "dissemination among the various colonising and colonised populations of the discourses that supported colonialism were also at their most extensive" (2–3).

By the second half of the twentieth century, the American empire, too, became an established global force, and its acquisition of Puerto Rico and the Philippines also set a new phase in US imperialist efforts. In short, a nascent modernism began to accelerate within a context of imperialist dominance, and the two major forces that would shape its trajectory—namely, the United Kingdom and the United States— would figure prominently in the works and artists of its canons.

As a pioneering work investigating colonialism's traumas, Martinican writer Frantz Fanon's *Black Skin, White Masks* (1954) explores what critic Sandra Courtman calls "the routine quality and defamiliarization of systematic tropes of violent colonial power structures" (32).[3] Postcolonial theorists of the second half of the twentieth century began to open the field (still young at the time) to thinking through multiple investments in art and aesthetics as being inextricably bound up in the complicated nexus of empire and ownership. Books like Edward Said's *Orientalism* (1978), Robert Young's *Postcolonialism* (2001), Sarah Brouillette's *Postcolonial Writers and the Global Literary Marketplace* (2007), and Graham Huggan's

The Postcolonial Exotic (2001) challenged scholars to recast old fields and theories within a new framework of power dynamics that resulted from conquest and imperial domination.

Because the region we now call the Caribbean was rife with competing agendas of national investments from Spain to the United Kingdom to France to the United States, analysis of it as a site of modernist inquiry must be accompanied by an examination of postcolonial traumas: "The nexus between that history and its traumatic legacy," Courtman continues, "is crucial to our understanding of Caribbean literature" (32). The Caribbean, then, exists as a contested site—politically, economically, and culturally—onto which various modernist social actors imposed their own interests and ideas about tradition. Raphael Dalleo starts his monograph *Caribbean Literature and the Public Sphere* (2011) by acknowledging the Caribbean's "multiple obstacles for literary history": we simply cannot locate the "traditional unity of the nation in a region comprised of more than a dozen national units; language provides no more stable of a ground, with literature from the Caribbean appearing in at least four imperial languages and a number of local languages" (1). The Caribbean's political and linguistic diversity transformed it into a critical space for modern artists to theorize possibilities for identifying race in comparison and contradistinction to their European models.

Caribbean writers such as José Martí, Stephen Cobham, and Jacques Roumain and Marie Vieux-Chauvet, meanwhile, present complex relationships to the colonial histories of their homelands (Cuba, Trinidad, and Haiti, respectively). More importantly, many of these writers explored means by which to speak back against imperialist demands and to advocate for anti-colonial measures.

The very process of "modern colonialism," Dalleo suggests, "enabled writers throughout the region to see themselves speaking for a national public as well as part of a counterpublic opposed to power" (69). These anti-colonial stances responded to "attempts to remove local power from the Caribbean" (69). A writer like Jamaican-born Claude McKay could, then, launch anti-colonial critiques in his homeland (at once a racial and national argument), while also agitating for more nuanced understandings of class dynamics. Dalleo reads McKay's 1933 novel *Banana Bottom* as an "anticolonial project" that is not primarily about "the casting off of Europe, but an examination of racial as well as occupational differences within the Jamaican middle class to make the case for the best form of leadership for the local nation" (100). As we will explore further—especially in our discussions of the Harlem Renaissance and of performance culture—the investments that came to typify modernism were always as political as they were aesthetic for artists and writers of color.

In the postcolonial novel *No Pain like This Body* (1972), Trinidadian-born writer Harold Sonny Ladoo explores colonial trauma in relation to the importation of more than 400,000 Indian laborers who came as indentured workers to the Caribbean. Critic Abigail Ward notes that the description of the Caribbean in Ladoo's novel as a "dangerous and hostile landscape" is in direct contradiction to European depictions of the region as "a paradisiacal tourist haven" (134). In this way, Ladoo presents a counter-narrative to European and American renderings, for, as Ward continues, "British colonial travel writers often praised the region's horticultural variety and the fertility of the land . . . yet, the beauty of the landscape that so dazzled colonial writers may distract from the reality of the region and the violent history of colonisation [*sic*], slavery and indenture" (134).

Saint Lucian poet and playwright Derek Walcott describes a similar imperial aesthetic aimed at eliding trauma in the region:

> An old map of the islands does not look like a cartography of imagined paradises, but like what they were in historical reality: a succession of crusted scabs with the curve of the archipelago a still-healing welt. No metaphor is too ugly for the hatred and cruelty the West Indies endured; yet their light is paradisal, their harbors and shielding hills, their flowering trees and windy savannas Edenic. ("A Frowsty Fragrance" 61)

For Walcott and Ladoo, then, the devastating effects of colonialism on Caribbean subjects take center stage in an ostensible paradise.

But the literary was not the only genre in which Caribbean artists attempted to speak to/against imperial powers. In her important monograph *Modernism, the Visual, and Caribbean Literature* (2007), Mary Lou Emery investigates the work of English-born visual artist Edna Manley, who later married her Jamaican cousin and moved to the island. Manley's artistic life changed with her move to the new territory, and she produced work directly inspired by the culture and people of her new island home. Emery especially analyzes the responses to the artist's 1922 sculpture, *Beadseller*, which is immediately consumed by a modernist artistic mindset as being informed first and foremost by a European aesthetic. "However," Emery concludes, "this inspiration, received from people of African descent, coincided with Manley's evident recognition of the power within a modernism that only appeared European, but was actually a configuration of forms and styles hybridized from European, Iberian, Egyptian, Asian, and to a very large extent, African sources" (71). Worth pointing out here, of course, is how a certain politics of proximity shapes a different reading of Manley by new modernist scholars than is extended to Picasso or Gaugin. A text is not rendered progressive or retrograde because of the subject matter itself but because of the power dynamics that surround its production and those that couch the scholarly analyses of it. Modernist (and new modernist) identifications of race, then, are more about the namers than the things being named.

Other, Othering

Another major point of interest for Hemingway was his exoticization of Cuban culture and his fetishization of its people. For Hemingway, Cubans were unlike any other people he had met during his travels across Europe, and their importance to his fiction relied on how he used them to represent another kind of identity that was not prominent to European and American audiences and writers. The empire/colony bifurcation necessarily stacks up a subject/object split that similarly reifies dominant discourses of power and obscures local histories, as well as social, cultural, and artistic enterprises. Booth and Rigby argue that "a major issue in the philosophy of modernity is the relation of self to other, and the power relations involved. The critique of modernity has involved examining how the modern subject was also an inherently 'colonising' subject" (3–4). In a conception of "other," as a literal definition—the notself—modernism made a movement out of examining a concept that was something of a paradox, for the philosophy of the movement required "the 'other' to be at once present and subjugated" (4). It is, therefore, no tremendous leap of logic to argue that many modernist artistic endeavors were "saturated to its core with colonialist attitudes" (4).

If we further tease out some of the core concerns of modern artists about analyzing their subject matter, we find more fingerprints of colonial anxieties. Booth and Rigby suggest as much:

> Doubts gathered around the project of empire, whether it could be sustained or was nearing its end. Was the racial and colonial "other" the barbarian at the door, to be resisted to preserve psychological security and cultural values? Or were they what offered an exhausted and tired West, its people and its literature a way out? Modernist writing often answered "yes" to both of these questions. (7)

Anxieties over the "racial other" permeated the works of modernist writers from E. M. Forster to William Faulkner and Joseph Conrad. In fact, one could argue that the othering of the colonial subject was key to the evolution of European and American modernisms alike. While the British empire, for example, exerted its prodigious political and military power over its colonies in the Caribbean, its imperial actors were not without fear of what the subjugated peoples of those territories might do in retaliation. Still a relatively recent memory, after all, was the Haitian Revolution, which resulted in the independence of the nation and the toppling of several of Europe's major military powers. Additionally, micro-revolts also contributed to questions about the stability of power dynamics in the region. The Morant Bay Uprising of 1865 resulted in the death of twenty white government officials. In response, the local governor, Edward Eyre, executed over four hundred Jamaicans and tortured hundreds more over the course of a sadistic stretch of thirty days. Robert Young notes in *Colonial Desire* that, in the aftermath of that uprising (and its brutal answer by Eyre), "the cultural ideology of race became so dominant that racial superiority, and its attendant virtue of civilization, took over even from economic gain or Christian missionary work as the presiding, justifying idea of the empire" (92).

We might connect this anxiety over potential uprisings with a broader anxiety over containment, registering dis-ease with literal disease. Fears of infection and contagions ran rampant at the time, and the colonial "other" often became a symbol for disease itself, a pernicious virus that could infect or wipe out the larger body politic.[4] Anxiety over infection also connected to fears about mixing of races and miscegenation. For example, Urmila Seshagiri notes that "the link between race, civility, and skull size captivated the popular imagination, perhaps best epitomized by the British craze for head measuring" (23). Playing off this obsession with "the racial semiotics of the skull and the head," Seshagiri argues that such a foundational text of modernism like Conrad's *Heart of Darkness* (1899) relies on a similar fear of "traveling to the savage, tropical Dark Continent [which] would negatively alter the structure of the head." Seshagiri locates similar anxieties over racial mixing and hybridity in Virginia Woolf's *Orlando* (1928), George Orwell's *Burmese Days* (1934), and Sir Arthur Conan Doyle's *The Hound of the Baskervilles* (1902).

Of course, an anxiety about a racialized other at the end of the nineteenth century has an important corollary in the national discourses in America spurred by the wake of the Civil War. What caused majority opposition to the idea of American expansion in the Caribbean in the wake of Reconstruction was a fear of the power it might offer newly freed blacks in the country. Peter Schmidt notes that these concerns were largely "racist" in nature, with southerners especially wringing their hands over "'colored' dependents." However, some advocated for the maintenance of an American foothold in the Caribbean "in part because they felt that the southern economy, especially cane and cotton growers and mill owners, would directly benefit" (106). In fact, the Caribbean became such an important site for American southern artists in the late nineteenth and early twentieth century that it found its way into many of the books now considered foundational to southern modernism. William Faulkner's Thomas Sutpen proves himself a man of value by quelling an uprising on a plantation in Haiti; Margaret Mitchell's Scarlett O'Hara is descended from French plantation owners who fled Haiti during the Haitian Revolution; and Zora Neale Hurston's *Tell My Horse* is, in the words of Leigh Anne Duck, a "blend of ethnography and travelogue . . . [that] castigates Caribbean social structures and praises the 1915–1934 U.S. occupation of Haiti" (127). Thus, the ways in which the Caribbean functioned as a site for "othering" in the "other South"—the American South—is worth considering.

The "Other South"

It is not a coincidence that Hemingway nicknamed his plot of land a "farm"; Cuba's agricultural history connected it to the West through a series of economic investments in the land. The capitalistic model of the plantation in imperial contexts figures prominently in the work of scholars who examine this important link between the Caribbean and the American South. In their special 2016 issue of *Global South*, editors Amy Clukey and Jeremy Wells investigate why the "plantation has proved one of the more durable signifiers of modernity" (2) and suggest a new field of study, one they term "plantation modernity." In such a field, Clukey and Wells feel the concept of the plantation

> increasingly seems inseparable from and even productive of key concepts of modernity, including theories of property and personhood; ideas about labor and its scientific management; ideals of liberty and contests over the meanings of "freedom"; impulses toward colonial control and anti-colonial resistance; and, of course, understandings of race, problems of the color line, and the evolving logics of state violence against brown bodies. (7)

Their approach to "plantation modernity" finds critical common ground with a variety of scholarly paradigms to imagine an "interdisciplinary field of study that takes a truly comparative, transnational look at the plantation as a global socioeconomic and cultural phenomenon" (8).

In exploring the implications of setting modernist projects on plantations, an immediate connection between the Caribbean colonies and the American South is easily made. In *American Creoles*, editors Martin Munro and Celia Britton remark on the connection between the "South" the "other" South, suggesting that the plantation is "the common matrix for the diverse nations and territories of the circum-Caribbean": "Such are the similarities that, when Édouard Glissant visited Mississippi and Louisiana, he found himself explaining to Americans the ways in which their world mirrored and echoed his own homeland of Martinique" (3). Indeed, returning to Glissant here is useful again because his scholarship offers connections between the Caribbean and the American South (as well as Latin America). His influence in postcolonial and post-structuralist scholarship in relation to modernism is evident, for example, in his 1996 work *Faulkner, Mississippi*.

The monograph Glissant produces ultimately is a different form of creolization than that employed by Brathwaite and Walcott with T. S. Eliot because it operates from a critical, rather than a creative, perspective. Hugues Azéradt finds powerful Glissant's move of "allowing the South, and the mythic county of Yoknapatawahpa, to establish itself in . . . the creolizing archipelago which stretches from South America to the shores of Louisiana" (200). In so doing, Glissant "take[s] a writer's work which had become mired in an increasingly individualizing and atavistic space and whose flagging universalism was denigrated by critics, and free it from its ghetto" (200). More importantly, by establishing Faulkner's connection to a transatlantic, and more specifically, Caribbean context, Glissant offers us what critic Michael Wiedorn calls a "poetics of paradox" in the "shared cultural zone made up of the Caribbean and the US Gulf South region" (183). Examining Faulkner's prominence in modernist canonicity, Glissant also claims him as "the genitor of a multilingual, pan-Caribbean poetics . . . [who] has *borrowed* the *language* of Faulkner's literary practice" (184).

Glissant's use of the South as a context for reconfiguring modernist frameworks is not a solitary endeavor. Rather, it is part of a much broader examination of the linkages between the Caribbean the American South—ones that are critical to new modernist studies. In Trinidadian author V. S. Naipaul's *A Turn in the South* (1989), for example, the writer decides to travel throughout the southern half of the United States to locate connections between the culture, architecture, and social life of its people and those of the world he grew up in as a child. Spending his time traversing the "deep South" of Mississippi, Georgia, Alabama, and Florida, Naipaul finds the people he meets resonating with his own perspective. While talking to a woman about class hierarchies in the American South, Naipaul notes,

> She was giving the view from below, the view of the poor people she was concerned about. And from what she said I got the impression that these people had raw sensibilities and lived on their nerves . . . I understood. Perhaps in a society of many groups or races everyone, unless he is absolutely secure, lives with a special kind of stress. Growing up in multiracial Trinidad as a member of the Indian community, people brought over in the late nineteenth and early twentieth centuries to work the land, I always knew how important it was not to fall into nonentity . . . in Belize in Central America, a similar feeling of the void broke through my other preoccupations when I saw the small, lost, half-Indian community of that wretched British colony, coastal timberland poached from what had been the Spanish Empire, peopled with slaves and servants, and then more or less abandoned: New World debris. (33)

In the "view from below," Naipaul notes the connection between identifications of race/class/nation in the American South and those in the Caribbean. Even more importantly, he posits the concept of being "below" as a shared identity marker unifying people in the two regions and creating a "New World debris." The debris metaphor is a constructive one, implicitly rejecting the very notion of a stable— even if shared—identity.

Important scholarship in recent decades has emerged on the connections between the South and the Caribbean, bringing the American region into a transatlantic context as well. Some examples include Frank Andre Guridy's *Forging Diaspora* (2010), which foregrounds the significance of Afro-Cuban connections with African American political projects; Philip Curtin's *The Rise and Fall of the Plantation Complex* (1998), which provides an analysis of plantation economies in a global context; and James Smethurst's *The African American Roots of Modernism: From Reconstruction to the Harlem Renaissance* (2011) and George Handley's *Postslavery Literatures in the Americas: Family Portraits in Black and White* (2000), both of which discuss post-slavery and post-Reconstruction racial identifications and performances. Additionally, scholars in southern studies (Leigh Anne Duck, Peter Schmidt, John T. Matthews, Jon Smith, and Deborah Cohn, just to name a few) have brought critical analyses of the South into hemispheric and transnational orbits with discussions of the "Global South."

Work on other souths often finds salient connections to, among other regions in the Caribbean, Cuba, inasmuch as the island was uniquely situated during the early part of the twentieth century as a stage on which notions of ethnicity and nationality were performed. It also served as a framework for an emerging dialectic of modernism and primitivism. "Cuba" has long existed as a site through which American and European imaginations have fashioned cultural desire in ambivalent ways. As "Cuba" became increasingly useful as a rhetorical framework for discussing themes of nation and identity, modernist formulations of race emerged through that same framework. When approached through the context of Cuba, modernist discourses of race and identity have striking implications for contemporary scholarly approaches to the geo-social category now called the Global South.

More broadly construed, though, the scope of scholarship widens to take stock of the Caribbean not simply as a distinct entity or an exceptional site that became a crucial lens for modernist aesthetics. Rather, the Caribbean can be seen as a point of contact, a discursive space in constant conversation with another crucial site of inquiry for modernism—the American South. This analytical turn has been pivotal in both new modernist studies and new southern studies. The examination of connections between both regions marks the latest development in a global or transnational turn in the two fields and offers possibilities for expanding and complicating conventional scholarly notions of each region.

Deborah Cohn's monograph *History and Memory in the Two Souths* (1999), for example, sees race as the nexus in which both regions share a history and perspective:

> As described by [William] Faulkner . . . and [Fernando] Ortiz, the commerce by means of which the South [and] the Caribbean . . . as a whole have gained access to the world system is inextricably bound up with the regions' racial dynamics. Blacks have sown, but they have reaped little benefit for themselves from a nature which

cannot balance the social equations governing their lives and their homelands' economies. (184)

Meanwhile, Peter Schmidt notes in his *Sitting in Darkness: New South Fiction, Education, and the Rise of Jim Crow Colonialism, 1865-1920* (2008), "Chinese laborers were imported to work the sugarcane fields of Louisiana following Caribbean plantation models" (106). And even more recently still, scholar John Lowe argues in his *Calypso Magnolia: The Crosscurrents of Caribbean and Southern Literature* (2016), "It is time for us to understand the South, its people, and, above all, the idea of the South as seen and expressed by its writers, as connected to the world in myriad ways, but in particular to that part of the world that is contiguous—the Caribbean" (10).

This shift in focus within southern studies reflects a turn to the geographically and figuratively "deeper" Souths reflected not just in the Caribbean but more southern still—in South America, Africa, and Latin America. Such scholarship is demonstrated in books such as Jessica Adams, Michael P. Bibler, and Cécile Accilien's *Just Below South: Intercultural Performance in the Caribbean and the U.S. South* (2007); Jon Smith and Deborah Cohn's *Look Away!: The U.S. South in New World Studies* (2004); and Martyn Bone's *Where the New World Is: Literature about the U. S. South at Global Scales* (2017). In many ways, the connection between the Caribbean and southern United States, a crucial part of the transnational turn in modernist and southern studies alike, resituated both regions from conversational outliers to central speakers in a global context. In the next chapter, we explore more directly the place of the American South in modernist rhetorics of race.

Thinking outward

To be sure, there are myriad examples beyond the Caribbean that reveal nation-states to be contingent, their boundaries contested. Important work has focused on indigenous populations, as well as postcolonial sites such as India, Ireland, and South Africa, just to name a few.[5] All of these contexts demonstrate the co-constitutive relationship between the identifications of race and modernism, and scholarship illuminating their political and intellectual histories is productive indeed. The analytical shift into "new modernist studies" invites us to reckon with the multitude of modernisms that had long been collapsed into a central concept—the European/American expatriate model of modernism that adhered to a linear artistic trajectory of its (predominantly white) canon. However, when scholars admit the contingency of those conventions and bring into discussion the sites of colonial contest, there are opportunities for incisive analysis of the social and economic consequences of the ways in which modernists operationalized various identifications of race. These complicated systems of classification not only affected aesthetic endeavors but also reified political hierarchies.

Postcolonial theory helps keep at the fore the Eurocentric ideological model that shaped a modernist canon. With this in mind, scholars can attend to canonicity as a political heuristic reflective of imperial dominance rather than as a neutral catalogue of aesthetic value. Part of the work of the new modernist studies, then, takes shape in efforts to locate various texts and performances outside hegemonic discourses. Moreover, postcolonial theory challenges the notion of race as a fixed metric and presents it instead as a nexus of traversal and transgression, a site for endless slippage and variation. In the chapter that follows, we will continue the discussion of the American South as a fruitful corollary to and extension of postcolonial emphases on contingency, variance, and revision.

Notes

1   For further reading on Ireland, see Eóin Flannery's *Ireland and Postcolonial Studies: Theory Discourse, Utopia* (2009), and for more information on colony/empire in Latin America, see Patricia Novillo-Corvalán's *Modernism and Latin America: Transnational Networks of Literary Exchange*.

2   American and European writers like Ernest Hemingway, Marcus Garvey, William Faulkner, Margaret Mitchell, Zora Neale Hurston, Langston Hughes, and Jean Toomer explored the possibilities of what the Caribbean offered as a site of modernist aesthetics. Meanwhile, Caribbean writers like Claude McKay, Eric Walrond, Junot Diaz, Julia Alvarez, Kwame Dawes, Claudia Rankine, Danielle Legros Georges, and Elizabeth Nunez began building their own canon.

3   Abigail Ward ed., *Postcolonial Traumas: Memory, Narrative, Resistance* (Palgrave, 2015).

4   For just one example of this vein of scholarship, see Sheldon Watts, *Epidemics and History: Disease, Power, and Imperialism* (Yale UP, 1997).

5   Len Platt's edited collection *Modernism and Race* (Cambridge UP, 2011) offers a few such discussions in its pages (such as Finn Fordham's essay on "Joyce, China and racialised world histories," Kaori Nagai's essay on Irish revivalism, and Platt's essay on "Germanism, the modern, and 'England'").

3

Re-turning South (Again): Renaissances and Regionalism

The story Zora Neale Hurston tells about Kossola (later known as Cudjo Lewis) in *Barracoon* has just as much to do with Africatown in Alabama as it does with Kossola's early life in Africa. Written a handful of years later, *Their Eyes Were Watching God* includes a depiction of the relationship between the American South and the Caribbean when Janie and Tea Cake work in the Everglades. The crucial role the South played in modernist projects was a result not of its own regional uniqueness but of its transnational and circum-Atlantic relationships. Martyn Bone notes this in his discussion of Hurston's emergence in the canon of southern literature after the early 1990s (long after her work received critical attention in African American studies, women's studies, and American studies), cautioning against a reading that would place her too squarely in agrarian notions of the South. What deserve careful consideration, Bone argues, are "the ambiguities and complexities that characterize Hurston's treatment of African American life and labor in the rural South" (753).

With these complexities in mind, perhaps it should come as no surprise that one of the most prominent American modern novelists of the twentieth century was a Mississippian. In writing about his "postage stamp" of a fictional county in the rural recesses of his home state, William Faulkner investigated the critical notion of how race defined region. With the character of Joe Christmas in *Light in August* (1932), Faulkner played with the idea of the "tragic mulatto," a character whose region identifies him based upon his racial "impurity." Faulkner's South keeps front and center the kinds of ambiguities Bone references and Hurston typifies—a region associated with American modernism precisely because of the anxieties and dissonances in relation to racial identification.

At exactly the same time in 1898 that the United States was beginning to explore its investment in expansion outward through its stake in the Caribbean and other sites (especially the Philippines), a similar discussion about ownership and region was taking place within its own borders. After the end of the Civil War in 1865, the American South's land and economy were decimated. Its major political and intellectual figures had been discredited by their association to a virulent apologia for the forced enslavement of Africans, and its place within the larger framework of the nation was unstable to say the least. A project of "Reconstruction" was in place, but the idea of reconstructing anything out of the ashes of a region deemed recalcitrant and treasonous was a matter of intense debate on the American political stage. It is during this time—the decades between 1870 and 1880—that the future of the South became a national problem.

Peter Schmidt notes that the rhetoric of "Reconstruction" offered a holistic ideal to reframe the region of the South in the image of the northern world: "Reconstruction's very name suggests a vision of total, not piecemeal, reform. . . . Reconstruction has a special place in our history as an experiment in creating a multiracial democracy that was rapidly repudiated by a majority only a few years after its adoption" (12). Schmidt argues that, despite a rejection of Reconstruction politics, the rhetoric of universal reform persisted and became itself another kind of imperialist tool, for "it became *the* prime model for U.S. colonial policies abroad" (13). In this chapter, we explore modernist anxieties over race in a region, the national conversations about which had much in common with those taking place in the late nineteenth century about the Caribbean. The connection between these "two souths" is not a superficial discourse about region but rather an entrenched and complicated relationship between race and ownership.

In this historical moment—when the South's future was debated and argued by American intellectuals and politicians who were also interested in expanding an empire—a similar gradual swell of southern art and literature reached a crescendo in the 1920s and the 1930s with an outpouring that has come to be called the Southern Renaissance. Like the suggestive "Reconstruction" rhetoric, "Renaissance" does its own classificatory work, presuming a rebirth of art and literature out of a space of barren darkness. Many of the writers associated with the movement—like Eudora Welty, William Faulkner, Allen Tate, and Flannery O'Connor—became crucial figures in the broader modernist canon as well. The supposed "renaissance" in the American South shared modernist investments in aesthetic experimentation, and, more importantly to our discussion here, southern writers explored in their work themes about identifications and anxieties regarding race. Specifically, anxieties over miscegenation, mixing, passing, violence, and whiteness proliferate in Southern Renaissance texts.

Within this key site of American modernism, Southern Renaissance texts and figures generatively presented racial representation as fraught and demonstrated the myriad complexities and variances therein. Simultaneously, however, they also entrenched dominant discourses about white empowerment and nostalgia. After all, this period also saw the rise of a virulent and violent Jim Crow era in which white supremacy was written into the laws, consequently subjecting African Americans to lynching, beating, kidnapping. Reconstruction-era rhetoric and policies gave fuel to a brand of nationalism that, Schmidt notes, both "justif[ied] Jim Crow at home and . . . persuad[ed] many skeptical Americans that the U.S. imperial destiny abroad meant the reconstruction of its newly acquired colonies, with special emphasis on limited suffrage rights and new educational systems" (13). In other words, a number of different dialogues surrounding the rights and responsibilities of nations to their colonial projects connect with discourses surrounding the problem of the American South throughout the early decades of the twentieth century.

Central to an understanding of how American expansionism and Reconstruction in the end of the nineteenth and beginning of the twentieth centuries is an examination of discourses surrounding "exceptionalism," a term operationalized toward both national and regional ends. At the opening of her foundational monograph for new southern studies, *The Nation's Region: Southern Modernism, Segregation, and U.S. Nationalism* (2006), Leigh Anne Duck notes that, in spite of its many contemporary shortcomings globally, "the theory of American exceptionalism has proved remarkably resilient" (1) and that "formulations of U.S. southern exceptionalism have been only slightly less tenacious" (2). We might trace a history of these rhetorics for both nation and region back to this historical moment of 1880–1920 when the South began to exert an artistic influence within modernist movements more broadly and when America began to position itself as a prodigious global power.

The American South at the beginning of the twentieth century has frequently been framed in terms of its backward or distinctly premodern mindset. That the region becomes a setting for writers and artists to work through the complicated integers of modernism might appear, on the surface, to be incongruous. Theories explaining the timing of this outpouring of art and literature often cite the disconnect between local (insider) and national (outsider) conceptions of the region. Looking to provide an origin story for the creative wellspring, Richard King offers several theories in his *A Southern Renaissance* (1980) as to why the region became the fertile territory for modernist initiatives, including his idea that "the Renaissance was the product of the creative tension between the Southern past and the pressures of the modern world" (4). In these narratives about the beginning of a "Southern Renaissance"—themselves a rhetoric of exceptionalism—critics frequently offer up the presumed mindset of "the southern artist." The features that shape this figure—decimated by the loss of shared ideals; scarred by the repeated tensions between economically and socially alienated nation and region; and burdened by an inescapable past with romanticized beauty—are emblematic of the conditions that animated the projects of modern artists across Europe as well.[1]

Such origin narratives collapse southern exceptionalism and a presumed modernist agenda in the South, facilitating white anxiety and upper-middle-class intellectual hand wringing while ignoring the ways in which these regional and racial classifications shaped Jim Crow legislation and public policy. However, a binary between America and "the South" should be resisted as well, inasmuch as it creates an easy and troubling definition of the region as the worst of American culture—what Duck describes as "an anomalous South [that] regularly displace[s] fundamental questions about political affiliation from discourse concerning the nation-state" (3). This rhetorical dichotomy allows America to be associated with "democracy and change and the region with racism and tradition" (3). Thus, the critical questions and terms in this chapter help us complicate regional classifications of the South, race, and nation. These representational efforts were ideological moves rather than neutral descriptions, demonstrating the co-constitutive relationship between aesthetics and politics. As such, they animated the crucible of modernism in America after the end of the Civil War.

Critical queries

In what ways has the South been posited both as distinctly anti-modern and as concomitant with modernist agendas, and what might this ambivalence suggest?

Though the conceptions of the South as "primitive" or backward flood much of the late nineteenth- and early twentieth-century descriptions of the region, we must not forget that, as discussed in the first chapter, modern writers and artists found in the so-called primitive a model for framing their own new traditions. Descriptions of southern modernism as being paradigmatic of a broader movement often cite the relevance of many core modernist tenets for the American South. In the wake of the loss of the Civil War, such assessments begin, there is something of the nascent disillusionment and fracturing of shared ideals that comes to Europe decades later in the period following the First World War. David A. Davis's recent monograph *World War I and Southern Modernism* (2017) argues that the prominence of such narratives dominated readings of the southern regionalism well into 1980s scholarship. The "mind of the South" (to borrow a dubious term coined by W. J. Cash) was steeped in modernist principles, and southerners' political, social, and economic losses left them susceptible to a movement that sought to explore alienation, moral relativity, decay and fragmentation, and anxiety. In fact, anxiety defined much of the world of southern whites, who were fearful of their shrinking power in the post-Reconstruction age and who displaced those fears onto southern African Americans.

How does the "South" function as a site in which modern artists work through white anxieties?

Many of the prominent figures of early southern modernism, and, indeed, the canon of southern literature, suffer from an unbearable whiteness of being. The primary way in which "race" appeared thematically in southern literature in the twentieth century has almost exclusively been to do with white anxieties about African American subjectivity.

One consequence of this emphasis, of course, was a narrow constituency for those included in what would become southern modernist canon. Further, representing the variety of southern art and literature primarily through the white titans of its increasingly bordered canon—for example, Faulkner, Welty, and O'Connor—has kept up and running a notion of southern discourse as primarily the terrain of white emotional fragility over perceived threats of racial otherness. Introduced in 2001 by Houston A. Baker, Jr. and Dana Nelson, "new southern studies" challenged the focus on white fragility that presented race as a "problem," charting a new course for the field in the process. Their approach deconstructed the notion of a monolithic white South, instead presenting the region as a series of narratives indexed according to multiple heuristics serving various interests. It also demanded a productive and significant analytical shift that would read "whiteness" as its own set of racialized power dynamics rather than as an invisible/ neutral norm. The category "race" that colonizers created to organize the economic investments of expanding empires was never meant to apply to them. This semantic rubric would continue to bear out centuries later in analyses that presented "race" as a synonym for "otherness." Baker and Nelson turn the tables on this configuration, bringing critical formulations of race as a rhetorical tool squarely into discussions about white writers that had presumed aesthetics, genre, and formal innovations to be topics removed from racial power dynamics.

How do white anxieties in the South over sexuality and miscegenation connect with modernist conceptions of bordered identities?
In the preceding chapter, we considered "hybridity" as a critical concept that animated modernist projects. It should come as no

surprise that modernist emphases on borders and crossings—both establishing and challenging them—would appear in texts coming out of the early twentieth-century American South. As Jim Crow laws legislated strict boundaries to keep African Americans segregated, anxieties over miscegenation and racial mixing grew. The borders that are most tenuous, of course, are subject to the most severe policing and provide the greatest opportunities for traversal. This idea had been borne out aesthetically in Europe already, as genre and form took dramatically different shapes. In the South, meanwhile, the policing of boundaries was playing out in violent ways. In the sections that follow, we will discuss the indissoluble ways in which ideas and laws—aesthetics and politics—shape one another. Renderings of anxiety, fear, hybridity, identity, race, and crossings in the twentieth-century American South collapse a would-be distinction between aesthetic and politics, ideology and power.

What does the idea of re-turning South offer us as scholars of modernism, and how does the region's "renaissance" connect with Harlem's?

In our final section, we will explore the concept of "renaissance," which has served as shorthand for modernist innovations both in the South and in Harlem. Following a blueprint established by Houston Baker,[2] we use his trope of re-turning to explore some of the conventional claims/ideas that scholars have long deployed in relation to the "Southern Renaissance" and the "Harlem Renaissance." Rather than present these monikers as descriptions of exceptional contexts, we see them as heuristic tools scholars have used to talk about, among other things, the role regionalism has played within the crucible of race and modernism. Key in the discussion of these connections is the idea that, in both cases, the work shared a reciprocal spatial significance. That is, in literal and symbolic ways, "Harlem" became an important site for southern African Americans, and "the South" was a critical region for Harlem artists. We will start our exploration by acknowledging the American South as a land of **lines** and borders, from those visible to those unspoken; from that bordered culture comes a series of **traditions** through which modernist writers like Faulkner interrogated the South's many conceptions of its **histories**, and how they influence culture.

Lines

Faulkner's Yoknapatawpha County is presented to readers as a map made up of lines and borders; while Faulkner maps the terrain physically, he also offers the invisible lines of segregation and policed identities as endemic to a culture that operates by keeping things crucially separated. White characters in his novels, such as Thomas Sutpen, refuse to acknowledge their heirs as legitimate when they are in any way mixed race; indeed, the tragedy of Sutpen's life is that he sets into motion a series of events that lead to his destruction all because he cannot legitimize his mixed-race son, Charles Bon. We begin our critical investigation of southern modernism and race with the concept of lines, both geospatial and metaphorical borders. Most broadly, the discursive move that specifies a South implicitly suggests a North. There is also the specific cartographic designation of the Mason-Dixon line to contend with. However, symbolic borders abound—W. E. B. Du Bois's "color line" being perhaps the most evocative example. It is this final border that we want to focus on more specifically inasmuch as southern modernists produced their work within a social and political system that highlighted the symbolic line between white and black. These writers responded to bordered and segregated structures with work that emphasized hybridity and interplay, transgressions and traversals. Those literary crossings—formative in Southern Renaissance canons—were reflective of and reflected by southern political and criminal codes.

Although a specific geospatial notion of "the South" coalesced near the beginning of the Civil War, a concept of a particular kind of southern regional monolith dates back much further than 1861. The Mason-Dixon line originated from a 1763 border dispute; in the drawing of the line, it divided the state of Pennsylvania from those below it: Maryland and West Virginia. By the next decade, however, it effectively segregated the states between those who had abolished the forced enslavement of Africans and those who allowed the institution to continue. The Mason-Dixon line took on new symbolic importance during the antebellum era, and in the postwar years, it bifurcated the nation into an easy binary between "the North" and "the South." In her 2009 monograph, *The Scary Mason-Dixon Line: African American Writers and the South*, Trudier Harris explores the symbolic weight that the "South" has for twentieth-century black writers as diverse as Raymond Andrews, Ernest J. Gaines, Edward P. Jones, Tayari Jones, Yusef Komunyakaa, Randall Kenan, and Phyllis Alesia Perry. Harris concludes that, regardless of African American authors' birthplaces, reckoning with the concept of the "South" is a rite of passage, if not a creative exorcism, that opens up foundational questions about identity/identification with a national history. However, like most geographies relying on imaginary and arbitrary borders, the South's importance became not so much about mapping as about narrativizing. Baker and Nelson describe that symbolic weight as central not just to the definition of the region but to that of the nation more broadly: "In order for there to exist a good union, there must be a recalcitrant, secessionist 'splitter.' To have a nation of 'good,' liberal, and innocent white Americans, there must be an outland where 'we' know they live: all the guilty white yahoos who don't like people of color" (235). If lines like the Mason-Dixon line create cartographic borders, Baker and Nelson make clear they also offer symbolic binaries that can be made to evaluate artistic, social, and cultural value.

As noted earlier, Leigh Anne Duck uses the model of the North/ South binary to think through literal and figurative segregations inflicted on the region. Starting with the notion of the South as a pernicious presence in American progressivism, she notes, "Long configured in U.S. discourse as a region removed from contemporary national culture, the South was increasingly seen, during the 1930s, as a threat to national economic and political structures" (18). Duck contends that the perceived threat of what was "down there" operated as a discursive fantasy of "disavowal" for narratives of US national identity in the twentieth century. If lines could separate systems of valuation, they also offered a mode of identification for deeming things valuable.

Segregation from the nation is foundational to the beginnings of a southern literary scene in the twentieth century not least because those (white) authors writing at the onset of the Southern Renaissance took their task to be answering for the region's artistic value in response to a maelstrom of critique from the nation at large. The first poets of southern modernism—Vanderbilt's Fugitives—were largely made up of remnants from an agrarian philosophical movement. Writing their infamous jeremiad, *I'll Take My Stand*, in 1930, the authors took as their subject the aesthetic defense of southern culture and art, the critique of which was most painfully leveled by a 1917 article entitled "Sahara of the Bozart" in the *New York Evening Mail* by H. L. Mencken, a prominent cultural critic in the 1920s. In the brief article, Mencken excoriated the poverty of the South, which, as he saw it, included not only economic distress but also intellectual and artistic vacuity:

> I leave it to any fair observer to find anything approaching culture in the South today. It is as if the civil war stamped out all the bearers of the torch and left only a mob of peasants on the field. In all that gargantuan empire there is not a single picture gallery worth going into, nor a single orchestra capable of playing a Beethoven symphony, nor a single opera house, nor a single monument or building (less than fifty years old) worth looking at, nor a single factory devoted to the making of beautiful things. . . . In such an atmosphere, it must be obvious, the arts cannot flourish. The philistinism of the emancipated poor white is not only indifferent to them; it is positively antagonistic to them. (7–11)

In their reaction to Mencken, the Agrarians of *I'll Take My Stand* attacked not only the binary of poverty/richness (by suggesting the South is the most culturally rich region of the nation) but also the line drawn by Mencken to define the region as hopelessly rural. It is useful to recognize that this debate between the Agrarians and Mencken— formulated so often in pedagogical and research models as *the* origin to the "Southern Renaissance"—was not centered on exploding the

binaries of North/South, black/white, poor/rich, urban/rural. Instead
it had as its prime directive contesting which part of the equation was
discursively valuable—an effort toward identifying "cultural value"
that was inevitably as theological as it was rhetorical.

As late as 1980, Richard King was offering that the "main interest
in *I'll Take My Stand* lies in its rendition of the Southern past. The
Agrarians' great good time was the antebellum South—a felicitous,
harmonious balance of yeomen and planter, culturally the bastion of
non-materialistic values, and economically opposed to the expanding
capitalism of the North" (55). Implicit in the Agrarians' creation of
the binary of past/present—and ultimate celebration of "the past"—
is the valuing of a past in which enslavement was "benevolent in
practice," and in which the war itself was "a betrayal by the North
of the compact hammered out at Philadelphia in 1787" (55). Thus
in the earliest phases of what became deemed "southern literature,"
lines did important work toward adjudicating social, regional, and
racial values.

Once drawn, lines are policed as a matter of social (and,
by extension, artistic) interest in making the ambiguity and
contingency of those lines appear natural and impenetrable. In
his *In the Shadow of the Black Beast: African American Masculinity
in the Harlem and Southern Renaissances* (2010), Andrew Leiter
examines one strand of policing of the color line that becomes
a central focus of much of southern modern fiction—the "fear
that 'blackness' was sneaking into the white race" (89). Such an
anxiety worked on a corporeal level—he notes that the obvious
way of detecting racial crossing was through "discernible racial
markings"—but the perceived danger operated more insidiously

on a metaphorical level because "there were numerous persons with African American ancestry who were capable of passing as white and bypassing the codes of segregation" (89). Once the threat of racial mixing moved from the realm of the physical to the symbolic, its weight became a major source of inspiration for southern authors, especially William Faulkner, perhaps the most prominent figure of southern literary modernism.

In novels such as *Light in August* (1932) and *Absalom, Absalom!* (1936), Faulkner presents characters in the South absolutely obsessed with/by the consequences of crossing racial lines and creating mixed-race populations of southerners. Some of his characters see the mixing as part of original sin, such as the abolitionist in *Light in August*, Calvin Burden, who says, "Damn, lowbuilt black folks: lowbuilt because of the weight of the wrath of God, black because of the sin of human bondage staining their blood and flesh. . . . They'll bleach out now. In a hundred years they will be white folks again" (234). Others, such as Shreve McCaslin in *Absalom, Absalom!*, imagine the process of miscegenation as a prelude to another kind of moral relativity in which nothing matters at all anymore. He says of the mulatto Jim Bond, "I think that in time the Jim Bonds are going to conquer the western hemisphere . . . as they spread toward the poles they will bleach out again . . . and so in a few thousand years, I who regard you will also have sprung from the loins of African kings" (471). But whatever the perspectives of his characters are, miscegenation remains a dominant theme for Faulkner's rendering of the South.

Leiter comments on Faulkner's paranoia over miscegenation, suggesting that, even in the author's conception of progress in which black culture gradually integrates into southern white spaces, "whiteness remains intact as the normative racial marker" (75).[3] While Faulkner's interest in miscegenation operates aesthetically as an exploration of duality and multiplicity, it nonetheless keeps up and running a white hegemonic rubric of racial identification. Leiter finds that such emphasis on whiteness is not shared with Faulkner's contemporaries, many of whom "offered alternative visions of racial mixing that rejected demagogic assertions of miscegenation as the deterioration of 'whiteness' and instead embraced notions of a mixed-race society as an imminent and progressive development for humanity" (76). As an example of the kind of work Leiter sees as productively employing tropes of hybridity and fluidity, he offers Jean Toomer's *Cane* (1923), wherein a "culture and population already thoroughly hybrid and so advanced in amalgamation as to render white and black obsolete were it not for . . . ongoing racial violence" (79).

The ongoing violence, of course, came as a result of the direct policing of racial borders imposed through the color line, and it demonstrates the ways in which a literary embrace of hybridity as an aesthetic tool was often a mode of experimentation available only to white authors. For Faulkner, lines may have segregated spaces, but they offered potential for play.[4] Modernist southern authors used lines not only to segregate spaces and ideas but also to exclude or disavow cultural and literary agents who identified with the region in ways they found problematic. In the next section, we explore lines as borders that authors and critics used to police their particular claims about modernism, especially in relation to binaries on tradition/experimentation and authenticity/artifice.

Tradition

Faulkner's fiction is replete with instances of characters operating out of a sense of duty or honor, only to find that code bankrupted by a powerful new flattening of meaning in relation to tradition. At the end of the story "Delta Autumn" in the collection *Go Down, Moses*, the old man Issac McCaslin scolds a mixed-race woman who comes to him expecting to have her love for Carothers, McCaslin's younger, white relative, requited. When he tells her to marry within her race, the woman scolds him back and suggests that he has lived too long to even remember what love is. Tradition holds McCaslin back from evolution, and he ends that story profoundly confused by the new hierarchy of the world surrounding him. Experimentation marked a key feature of modernism, and yet, for there to be some form or structure to experiment with, there first had to be a point of departure, a port of call, a place to move from. In his essay "Tradition and the Individual Talent," Eliot suggested as much:

> We shall often find that not only the best, but the most individual parts of [a poet's] work may be those in which the dead poets, his ancestors, assert their immortality most vigorously. What happens is a continual surrender of himself as he is at the moment to something which is more valuable. The progress of an artist is a continual self-sacrifice, a continual extinction of personality. [. . .] The more perfect the artist, the more completely separate in him will be the man who suffers and the mind which creates. (75)

This emphasis on tradition—in form, mode, ideal, and cultural/social actions—was fundamental to the work of artists and writers at the time in the American South.

The poets from Vanderbilt, known collectively under the name "Fugitives," assembled within the aforementioned Agrarians, the collective authors of *I'll Take My Stand* (1930). King notes of both the Fugitives/Agrarians that their membership blossomed in large part out of a defense of southern traditions: "As the Southern tradition loomed problematic after World War I, a not uncommon reaction was to defend it all the stronger, shearing it of what little complexity it possessed" (52). While the Agrarians defended southern (agri)cultural and political traditions, Fugitive poets began, in their poetry, to "advance . . . a more sophisticated version of the Southern family romance. Gentility was replaced by veneration of aristocracy; nostalgia was given added bite by combativeness" (52).

In their efforts to reify and celebrate "southern tradition," both the Fugitives and Agrarians argued for a literary criticism that took an historical and "professional" approach, consequently judging art with a metric that elided historical, biographical, and cultural contexts. For southern artists—attacked for a poverty of intellect—such an argument not only represented a welcome relief from readings of their work that invited critics to investigate their relationship to region and its politics but also provided the opportunity for the poets to entrench their work in the very tradition within which they located (and simultaneously manufactured) themselves. The resulting literary critical paradigm—dubbed "New Criticism" by the first author to promote its potential for revolutionizing literary criticism, John

Crowe Ransom—positioned the poetic object in a way that Eliot would approve.

And yet, New Criticism's emphasis on the poem's importance on its own terms, as "an order of existence," to borrow Ransom's phrasing, stressed in decidedly un-modern ways tradition over formal experimentation. King argues that Ransom's main idea in the formulation of New Criticism was to assert that "the critic should concern himself with the *forms* at work in the poem, handed down by the tradition" (67, emphasis in original). For Ransom, the tradition was one given by the "old society—the directed and hierarchical one" (67). Claiming a poem's value is based on its relationship to a tradition (discursively invented by Ransom and later reified through his emphasis on artistic endurance) is troubling for the contemporary post-structuralist critic, not least because an evolution of criticism reminds us that "inheritance" and "heritage" are their own rhetorical heuristics that have a history, not an "order of existence." As Scott Romine argues in the opening of his *Real South: Southern Narrative in the Age of Cultural Reproduction* (2008), the Fugitives emphasized an "inheritance and tradition grounded in the economy of an agrarian society" (5), but the very model they promoted was an invention. Lewis Simpson concludes in his *The Man of Letters in New England and the South: Essays on the History of the Literary Vocation in America* that "much of [the Fugitive/Agrarian's] inheritance is artifice," and "no American writers ever worked harder at inheriting their inheritance than the Agrarians" (248)." The turn of New Criticism was a turn toward Eliot's tradition—focused adjudication of modernist poetry— with a particular emphasis on ontological essence that functioned both poetically and pedagogically.

Ransom and his cohort invented a mode of criticism that not only offered a prescription for artistic judgment and value but also gave the literary world a paradigm that did implicit political work. In the words of King, Ransom spends much of his time honing New Criticism through "incessant and insistent polemicizing against liberal and radical tendencies to read literature as a set of proposals for future social orderings or to reduce literature to sociological determinants" (66). Such a political viewpoint not only established New Criticism as a deeply conservative movement in literary criticism but also promoted a critical perspective that was used to entrench a canon based on already dominant hierarchies of value. This approach formulated the "poetic" as an ahistorical phenomenon with the assistance of concepts like "inheritance" and "tradition." In the process, however, it also allowed only a very narrow constituency access to the ostensible tradition of southern intellectual history. Predictably, African American southern artists and literary figures were particularly affected by this oversight in Fugitive/Agrarian/New Critical projects.

It would take decades for writers of color to be included within a regional modernist tradition. Of little wonder, then, is that not until Fred Hobson's 1991 book *The Southern Writer in the Postmodern World* would there be an argument for African Americans' places in a canon of southern literary studies. It would take another ten years for Trudier Harris's memoir *Summer Snow: Reflections from a Black Daughter of the South* (2003) to be published, wherein Harris proclaims: "I am a Southerner. For a black person to claim the South, to assert kinship with the territory and the mores that most black folks try to escape, is about as rare as snow falling in

Tuscaloosa during dog days. It's a reconciliation that many African Americans have not yet made" (177). The relationship Harris notes between regional representation and racial representation is a direct byproduct of the implicitly white phenomenon of tradition that the Fugitives/Agrarians/New Critics promoted during the first three decades of the twentieth century. Their emphases on tradition suggested a particular mode of literary inheritance and lineage based upon a nostalgic relationship to a cherished past. As Harris demonstrates, however, these emphases also overlooked the histories and aesthetic forms of people of color—histories and forms from which, in many cases, those canonical texts drew for their own purposes.

In her short (a mere ninety-one pages) but significant book *Playing in the Dark: Whiteness and the Literary Imagination* (1992), Toni Morrison offers a critical examination of what she calls an "Africanist presence" that has been key, in her reading, to the construction of literary notions of "Americanness." Framing her discussion with readings of works by Edgar Allan Poe, Herman Melville, Willa Cather, and Ernest Hemingway, Morrison pulls back the curtain on modernist American ideals of individualism, freedom, manhood, tradition, and discovery, among others. In so doing, she reveals such notions as heavily reliant on (indeed, built upon) an oppressive racial power structure that creates the space for writers and scholars to naturalize that very structure by ignoring concerns of racial identifications in the pursuit of "humanistic" paradigms. The result of such an approach strikes a powerful blow to the presumed distinction between "text" and "context" (popular among New Critics, of course, but still easily found in contemporary scholarship).

Morrison describes her motivation and method in characteristically evocative fashion, through the useful metaphor of a fishbowl:

> As a writer reading, I came to realize the obvious: the subject of the dream is the dreamer. . . . It is as if I had been looking at a fishbowl—the glide and flick of the golden scales, the green tip, the bolt of white careening back from the gills; the castles at the bottom, surrounded by pebbles and tiny, intricate fronds of green; the barely disturbed water, the flecks of waste and food, the tranquil bubbles traveling to the surface—and suddenly I saw the bowl, the structure that transparently (and invisibly) permits the ordered life it contains to exist in the larger world. In other words, I began to rely on my knowledge of how books get written, how language arrives; my sense of how and why writers abandon or take on certain aspects of their project. I began to rely on my understanding of what the linguistic struggle requires of writers and what they make of the surprise that is the inevitable concomitant of the act of creation. What became transparent were the self-evident ways that Americans choose to talk about themselves through and within a sometimes allegorical, sometimes metaphorical, but always choked representation of an Africanist presence. (17)

This challenge—to look critically at social containing/enabling structures that so often seem invisible by virtue of the normalizing efforts of dominant groups—is key to new modernist returns to canonical works.

Romine's *Real South* investigates the explosion of narratives created on behalf of southern "tradition" that, deploying rhetorical markers of authenticity, delineated what came to be defined as unique to the region and, as such, authoritative. Taking his cue from Walter Benjamin's 1936 essay "The Work of Art in the Age of Its Technological Reproducibility," Romine argues that any conception of the "solid South" as an ontologically cohesive and stable site is simply a series of reproductions authorized by "the intervention of narrative" (9). Those narratives are operationalized to present a "real" or "authentic" version of a region even now in an age "increasingly dominated by mass media, global corporations, and the logic of commodification" (2). All the while, as in the case of the texts Morrison examines, their authors often ignore the figures and frameworks of racial and regional otherness on which they rely. In this way, the relationships (or the lack thereof) between writers and their sociopolitical contexts became a dominant trope of southern modernism.

Histories

The work of a quintessential southern modernist author like William Faulkner offers a rich case study for exploring these dynamics further. Faulkner's complicated oeuvre orbits around one central idea: the inability of his characters to escape fully the consequences of their (personal/cultural/social/inherited/regional) histories. In fact, one of the ways in which Faulkner works so well as a symbolic arbiter of modernism is that he fully embraces the modernist obsession with the wound of the past and the futility of attempts to move forward, transcend, or take revenge on what has already transpired. In what has become almost a slogan for modernist aesthetics, Faulkner's quotation from *Requiem for a Nun* appropriately sums up the author's engagement with history and its bearings on the present: "The past is never dead. It's not even past" (73). Faulkner's interest in the elusive present lost in the endless work of the past is not just a key theme in his novels; it is one of the foundational tenets of an ethos of southern modernism.

One of the most important modern historians of southern culture, C. Vann Woodward, coined a similar slogan when he defined the world of regional nostalgia as "The Burden of Southern History" in 1960. One cannot help but connect Woodward's phrase to another burden articulated close to the turn of the century by Rudyard Kipling, "The White Man's Burden." Jeremy Wells effectively connects both imagined "burdens" for white southerners in his *Romances of the White Man's Burden: Race, Empire, and the Plantation in American Literature, 1880–1936* (2011). He argues that the "plantation" itself was a site that reminded America—and especially the American South—of its troubled history, even as it also "came to seem, to many, a miniature version of present-day 'America'" (4). While the plantation is of specific interest to Wells here, his point applies more broadly to modernist formulations of southern regionalism as a crucible of economic, historical, and racial ambivalence.

Weighed down by the burdens of both a troubled/troubling history and a presumed charge to protect, "civilize," and "uplift" the nonwhite peoples of the world through imperialist enterprises, southern (white) writers loaded their work with tropes of both memory and teleology. Faulkner especially presented characters who were so weighed down with the burden of their pasts that they could not function in the modern world. The "hero" of both *The Sound and the Fury* and *Absalom, Absalom!*, Quentin Compson becomes so obsessed with maintaining a sense of a static present that he attempts to stop time by ripping the hands from his watch—a gift from his father, who, when he gives it to him tells him,

> I give you the mausoleum of all hope and desire. . . . I give it to you not that you may remember time, but that you might forget it now and then for a moment and not spend all of your breath trying to conquer it. Because no battle is ever won . . . . They are not even fought. The field only reveals to man his own folly and despair, and victory is an illusion of philosophers and fools. (*The Sound and the Fury* 48)

The burden of history coalesces into Faulkner's fictional world as a burden of memory, too. In *Light in August*, for example, one of his characters literally shares her family name with the word to describe their family's unbearable history: Joanna Burden. The daughter of a zealous abolitionist, Joanna is schooled from an early age about the "curse" of her southern heritage and how such history creates another burdensome charge to be responsible for the uplifting of a race her people sought to subjugate.

The obvious corollary to an obsession with burdensome histories is the focus within southern modernist works on memory. In *Light in August*, for example, Faulkner moves from narration of plot to a stream-of-consciousness meditation on how memory is related to knowledge when he begins a chapter: "Memory believes before knowing remembers. Believes longer than recollects, longer than knowing even wonders" (119). An emphasis on remembering as a kind of ontological effort becomes critical for southern authors in the twentieth century. Additionally, their interest in how memory obscures or elides various histories connects to broader modernist themes. Cohn notes in *History and Memory in the Two Souths* that the southern writer's location of a "crisis point in history . . . and the resulting perception of discontinuities between past and present . . . were also encoded in literary modernism, which was in part a response to the inability of modern civilization's deities of reason, order, and logic, to explain events in a war" (23). The gaps between reality and memory, and the narrativizing efforts that collapse the two into what becomes accepted as history, are crucial integers in explaining both a southern and a modern artistic ethos in the twentieth century.

Finally, these dissonances between fact and fantasy prove essential to one of the more stylized southern modern genres—the southern gothic novel. In *The Palgrave Handbook of the Southern Gothic* (2016), editors Susan Castillo Street and Charles Crow connect the rise of the genre itself to the region's troubled history: "The Southern Gothic is a genre that arises from the area's often violent and traumatic history" (2). But the term also relates to the lines of divisions we discussed above, for, as Teresa Goddu notes, "the American South serves as the nation's 'other,' becoming the repository for everything from which the nation wishes to disassociate itself. The benighted South is able to support the irrational impulses of the gothic that the nation as a whole, born of Enlightenment ideals, cannot" (qtd. in Street and Crow 2). With their emphases on decay and haunted spaces, southern gothic novels remind us that the region of the American South represents a site through which memory and history are continually and cyclically introduced into the present. Beyond being a genre of ghosts and spirits, southern gothic texts routinely engage in the techniques popular with modern authors of other regions and nationalities in their use of experimentation with "perspective and challeng[ing of] traditional representations of time. Linearity, causality, and chronological order are rejected and, instead, one finds events evoked, revived, and relived at memory's whim, as well as unmarked transitions between past, present, and future" (Cohn 23).

These southern histories find resonances in for contemporary work happening in the field of southern studies. For example, Martyn Bone's *Where the New World Is: Literature about the South at Global Scales* (2018) investigates "contemporary fiction—from 1980 to 2014—most of it by or about immigrants—[which] has resituated the U.S. South globally," but, Bone offers that this history is not "new" because "earlier twentieth-century writing already had done so in ways that traditional literary studies tended to ignore" (ix). If we teased out a notion above of how "tradition" operated for southern artists during the early twentieth century, we must also begin to query how "tradition" operates in an ethos of southern literary studies itself. For Bone, as well as for a generation of contemporary southern scholars engaged in "new southern studies," the hinge between breaking from a "traditional literary study" of the South and a "new study" of the region largely involves the animating concepts of racial/ethnic/national identities. Traditional southern studies worked through a fairly bordered and canonized world of white southern authors and busied itself with piecing together the aesthetics of its writers' anxieties over racialized burdens and histories. Analytical interventions like new southern studies and new modernist studies, however, challenged scholars to resist simply replacing one history with another. The ostensible stability of a narrative can be just as problematic as its particular substance.

Bone notes that, even though new scholarship emphasizes a
transnational approach to investigating the South (and, he offers,
modernism itself), scholars must be clear that the South's transnational
exchanges predate the opening of the field in the early twenty-first
century: "the region has always—even before it became what we call
the 'U.S. South'—been inextricably bound up with transnational
trends and processes" (xii).

Thinking outward

As stated at the outset of this chapter, a theoretical "re-turn" to the
South should not be taken to suggest that southern literary modernism
is a particular exemplar within a study of race and (new) modernisms.
Long after Malcolm X proclaimed that "Mississippi" existed in any
territory south of the border that the United States shares with Canada,[5]
scholars began exploring regional sites as ideological signifiers. In his
important monograph *Turning South Again: Re-thinking Modernism/
Re-reading Booker T* (2001), Houston Baker makes clear that such
projects go a long way toward engaging in the critical work of
"liberating black modernism" (10). Baker cautions, however, that even
new modernist revisions must nonetheless recognize that "almost
any given Afro-American historical configuration of people and
events defined as 'modernism' is . . . almost immediately historically
discredited by continuous, fully documentable white American
protocols of enslavement, criminalization, and punishment—the
unceasing derogation of the black-South body" (90).

Just as the past "isn't even past," then, the South isn't even southern
inasmuch as the region has long served as a metaphor for American
tabulations of race and modernity.

"One might say that *being framed* for the black American is being indexed by—and sometimes *in* the South," Baker argues (18). Thus, any productive analysis of "race and new modernism" cannot simply look for traditional (white) modernist themes in works by people of color. Instead, as previously mentioned, "race" and "modernism" must be understood as rhetorical tools that do important work in various attempts at organizing social worlds. What Baker calls for in his revisionary *Turning South Again* is the new term of "Afro-modernity," which "might be considered as a project in style, resistance, organization, art, literacy, and spirituality that surfaces from, say, Atlantic depths and holds, stretching from at least the fifteenth century to the phantasmagorical transformations of the South Africa in the 1990s" (34). The "endless haunting" of Booker T. Washington and his strategy of southern accommodation performance animates Baker's re-turn to the South, a region embedded in the very mythos of American—and even global—modernisms.

Taking seriously the questions social theory would have scholars ask about structural power dynamics and mobilizing rhetorics, productive investigations of conceptual monikers "race" and "modernism" in narratives in/about the "South" are imperative to new modernist moves within southern studies. The implications of such an approach for analyses of discourses on white aesthetics, masculinity, class exploitation, immigration, and authenticity—no matter the particular region or data set—are manifold indeed. Inasmuch as "the subject of the dream is the dreamer" (to borrow Morrison's phrasing), our points of entry reflect as much about our approach as they do about our topic. We are interested in, for example, preoccupations with regionalism, dialect, racial uplift, and urban/rural binaries—all analytical starting points rather than descriptive ends—that reveal rhetorics of race and modernism to be co-constitutive. Turning in the next chapter from one region to another—from South to North, from rural to urban—we apply this approach to the much-studied Harlem Renaissance.

Notes

1   In addition to King, other scholars who have written in this vein include Cleanth Brooks (see particularly *An Approach to Literature* and *Understanding Poetry*) and C. Vann Woodward (see *The Burden of Southern History* and *Origins of the New South, 1877–1913*).

2   See his book *Modernism and the Harlem Renaissance* (1987), which we discuss at length in Chapter 4.

3   Leiter, Andrew B. "Miscegenation and Progression: The First Americans of Jean Toomer and William Faulkner," in *Faulkner and the Black Literatures of the Americas*, Jay Watson and James G. Thomas, eds. (Oxford: U of Mississippi P, 2016), 74–88.

4   Important to keep in mind is that this was not the case for modernist African American southerners who were not afforded the same aesthetic opportunity, of course.

5   Malcolm, X., *By Any Means Necessary; Speeches, Interviews, and a Letter*, George Brietman, ed. (New York: Pathfinder Press, 1970, 1985), 81–82.

4

The Art of Ideology: Black Aesthetics and Politics in Modernist Harlem

Despite being born in Alabama and raised in Florida, and despite placing so many of her creative and anthropological interests in the South, Zora Neale Hurston has long been best known as a Harlem Renaissance writer. Her presence in the canon of southern literature did not take shape until the 1990s, around the same time that scholars expanded the concept of an erstwhile landlocked "South" to take stock of its position in transatlantic and Caribbean contexts. Pedagogically speaking, however, readers continue to come to know Hurston through and associate her most immediately with the period of artistic and intellectual innovation in 1920s and 1930s Harlem. This is understandable enough, of course. Hurston provides an easy proxy for the debates and themes prevalent in Harlem at the time regarding the role of African American artists and writers in the

ever-modernizing United States. Well-rehearsed are the entrenched
disagreements that took place over literary style and use of "dialect,"
her falling out personally and professionally with Langston Hughes,
and some of the high-profile negative responses to *Their Eyes Were
Watching God*. Richard Wright claimed dismissively[1] that Hurston
seemed to have no plans to attempt "serious fiction," and Ralph
Ellison called the novel "a blight of calculated burlesque."[2]

Hurston is often cast in contradistinction to her male literary
counterparts in the service of biography—illuminating and bringing
to life the personalities of figures who have consolidated places in
the Harlem Renaissance canon. These moments and events that
add dimension to various personae, however, are more telling as
reflections of the interrelationships between race and modernism,
politics and aesthetics. The importance of Harlem during that crucial
period of modernist thought and production cannot be overstated;
however, as with our other sites of analysis, the Harlem Renaissance is
not an exceptional end in itself but is instead productively illustrative
of the ways in which "race" and "modernism" came into relief by way
of each other.

Beginning a discussion of a phenomenon that has already received
so much scholarly attention warrants a bit of critical troubleshooting
from the outset. Offering the Harlem Renaissance as an emblem of
race in modernism runs the risk of implicitly offering an origins
narrative about the genesis of formal and thematic experimentations
in African American art. As discussed in the preceding chapter,
the label "renaissance" should be considered as well, inasmuch as
it presents a European model of reading literary/artistic value onto
cultural products. And, finally, positioning a movement within a
specific region during a particular historic moment unavoidably

distills in reductive ways the work black artists were doing during other decades and/or in other places. As scholars interested in discourses on race and modernism, we want to avoid these analytical hazards in our own discussion of the period that came to be known as the Harlem Renaissance.

Like any historical endeavor that aims to locate (and, inevitably, impose) beginnings, tracing an origin for a renaissance in Harlem is tricky. After all, the city was only one among many urban centers to which African Americans travelled upon leaving the South post-Reconstruction. Other cities—Detroit, Chicago, Baltimore, and others—offered similar prospective economic and civic opportunities for black citizens escaping the Jim Crow South, but none of them coalesced quite as identifiably as did the artistic community that Harlem nurtured in the early twentieth century. Initially a space for middle-class families who wished to live in the suburbs of Manhattan, Harlem saw its population change rapidly in the late nineteenth century as a tremendous swell of immigrants from Europe began to live in the borough. During the tumultuous time of the First World War, mass immigration to America paused; this short break in the expansion of immigrant communities in New York City meant that Harlem became known more as an African American enclave than as an "immigrant" one. As a part of the "Great Migration"—a term given to the mass migration of millions of African Americans from the South to the urban centers of the Midwest and Northeast—Harlem loomed large as a center in a major urban city that promised economic advance and community for African Americans throughout the nation.

Thus, Harlem became a major center for African American art and political philosophy for a variety of different reasons. George

Hutchinson notes as much in his book *The Harlem Renaissance in Black and White* (1995):

> The Harlem Renaissance followed not only (as is often stressed) the black migration and World War I but also the emergence of a whole new matrix of magazines centered in New York City. . . . Significantly, before the teens, these magazines either did not exist or were under the control of more conservative editors, a fact that has a lot to do with the timing of the Harlem Renaissance. (126)

Meanwhile, Shane Vogel emphasizes the explosion of nightlife and clubs around the borough as a galvanizing influence. In his book *The Scene of Harlem Cabaret* (2009), Vogel investigates the "function of Harlem's nightlife . . . [as] a critique of normalizing narratives of racial and sexual identity" (5). The varied reasons for what would become Harlem's dominance in African American modernisms suggest the need, then, for nuanced renderings of the site as constituted by multiple and competing interests rather than as an uncontested element in modernist canon.

African Americans migrating out of the South after Reconstruction set to the difficult task of debating what an enfranchised and participatory presence in the United States might look like and how to best achieve it. Identifying this task as the beginning of a discussion about the place of African Americans in a modern society and economy, Houston A. Baker, Jr., argues in *Modernism and the Harlem Renaissance* (1987) that the "commencement of Afro-American modernism [is] September 18, 1895 . . . [and Booker T.] Washington's delivery of the opening address at the Negro exhibit of the Atlanta Cotton States and International Exposition" (15). Baker calls this speech an origin inasmuch as it is the first moment in which "an agreed upon . . . direction was set for a mass of black citizens who had struggled through the thirty years since emancipation buffeted on all sides by strategies, plans, hopes, and movements, organized by any number of popular, or local, black spokespersons, without before 1895 having found an overriding pattern of *national* leadership" (15). The coalescing of a national conversation around the possibilities for an African American place in a modern American conversation in 1895 created political and philosophical frameworks for the notion of "uplift" that was central to the Harlem Renaissance's evolution.

This cross dialogue about how African Americans might gain a respectable foothold inside the modern United States served as a foundation for the artistic, literary, musical, and political projects that emerged in Harlem. This enterprise was the engine for artistic and intellectual trajectories in that context, sparking intense debates about what and how to build upon that foundation. Baker suggests that Booker T. Washington's philosophical and oratory performances, his "liberating manipulation of marks and a revolutionary *renaming,*" were foundational to an "Afro-American modernism" (25). However, Washington's suggestion for economic enfranchisement before civic and intellectual enfranchisement drew a strong rebuke from black intellectual leaders such as W. E. B. Du Bois, who Baker notes, "With stunning wit, sarcasm, and irony . . . records the 'narrowness' of Washington's leadership ideals, as well as the tangible retrogression (the 'descent,' as it were, to more abject depths than slavery) of the black 'country districts' under the banners of the Tuskegee institute" (83). While the Tuskegee project in Alabama does not figure prominently into our discussion of a modernist moment in Harlem, it is important to

note the backdrop for the debates animating the Harlem Renaissance—
inside of which the Tuskegee institute played a vital role.

The exchanges by/for African American artists and intellectuals
over how to establish themselves within the new national order of
the twentieth century—the results of which constitute the movement
that came to be called the Harlem Renaissance—prove significant
across a variety of academic fields, including anthropology, dance,
poetry, music, theater, political discourse, magazine cultures, fiction,
biography, to name only a few. These multifaceted approaches
demonstrate the array of creative and analytical possibilities contained
within this data set, as well as the problems with any scholarly attempt
to provide an exhaustive account of it. Inasmuch as there is simply no
way to document in one book, let alone one chapter, the varied and
dizzying reaches of the Harlem Renaissance, we want to identify in our
own discussion some of the points of contestation and collaboration
that forged a discourse on race and modernism in which aesthetics and
politics were inextricable. In the "Critical queries" section, we ask some
guiding questions that emphasize the movement's heuristic rather than
historical importance, and in the critical terms that follow, we highlight
major themes and ideas that contribute to such an emphasis.

Critical queries

*Why and how did Harlem animate notions of urbanity and
cosmopolitanism for modern African American artists?*
As already mentioned, Harlem is but one site that existed as an
ostensible urban oasis for African Americans. However, Harlem

functioned somewhat differently from other city centers in that prospects of economic advance were accompanied by equally vibrant artistic possibilities. New York City was the publishing capital of the United States, and major periodicals like *Crisis* and *Opportunity* emerged with the aim of exploring black life in the new modern era. New York became understood both in the United States and around the world as *the* destination in America for cosmopolitan lifestyles and artistic innovation. Art dealers, editors, patrons, major intellectuals all made New York City their home, and, at the turn of the century, the city provided opportunities for writers and artists looking to break into a bustling artistic or literary scene. While Philadelphia could offer the chance for economic mobility, and while Tuskegee advanced possibilities for vocational training, Harlem animated notions of artistic and intellectual community within the largest metropolis in the United States. It is no wonder, then, that so many artists and writers made Harlem their home; the borough offered to many African Americans a destination for both physical and symbolic escape.

How does the Harlem Renaissance complicate the relationships among ideas about artistry, ownership, and authorship?

While the temptation remains in contemporary scholarship to take for granted the places of Harlem Renaissance writers and artists in a modernist canon, the dominant legal structures that denied African Americans agency and safety in the early decades of the twentieth century created a context in which the status of these works were anything but inevitable. Many of the major figures associated with the Harlem Renaissance—authors like Zora Neale Hurston, Langston

Hughes, and Countee Cullen, for example—relied on the patronage
of white intellectuals, artists, and wealthy investors to promote their
work. White socialites and known intellectuals like Carl Van Vechten,
A'Leilia Walker, and Charlotte Osgood Mason would offer both their
financial and intellectual support to promote the works of African
American artists and writers and give them the tacit seal of authority
that would introduce them into the white literary and artistic worlds of
New York City. The ubiquity of the patronage system poses problems
for scholarship that would attempt to fashion a narrative about an
artistic community in Harlem that welcomed African Americans
with open arms and provided a liberating oasis of racial harmony. A
priority for new modernist scholars has been to give attention to the
complicated nexus of economic and political power dynamics that
forced many black artists and writers to rely upon white acceptance
for public exposure. In even more basic ways, these dynamics also
trouble the waters of an unambiguous Harlem Renaissance canon
because of the overt efforts by white patrons to manufacture authority
and aesthetic value in ways that suited their own priorities.

*Through themes like "passing," how did Harlem Renaissance writers
treat the societal and legal importance of presumed visual signifiers
of race?*

After the Civil War, legal codes that created a concept called "race"
in the first place were adjusted to accommodate emancipation while
keeping slave-era social hierarchies up and running.[3] Laws entered a
new taxonomic phase after the Reconstruction so as to draw perimeters
especially around racial ambiguity. For example, the 1822 legal standard
in Virginia that assigned the designation "mulatto" to people who had

one-quarter African ancestry changed dramatically over the course of the subsequent hundred years. Not long into the twentieth century, a mulatto was anyone with one-sixteenth African ancestry, and by 1924, under the Racial Integrity Act, people were "colored" according to the law if they had any African ancestry at all. This so-called "one-drop rule" relied heavily on visual signifiers, creating conditions in which racially ambiguous people were put in positions wherein they decided whether or not to "pass" for white and receive the many social/ economic/political benefits that came along with the designation. The phenomenon of passing and its consequences for the individual and the community alike was a theme taken up in the Harlem Renaissance as writers attempted to negotiate life in white America. Two of the most famous examples, both of which helped create the "tragic mulatto" archetype, are James Weldon Johnson's *The Autobiography of an Ex-colored Man* (first published anonymously in 1912 and then released again with author credit in 1927) and Nella Larsen's *Passing* (1929). Both narratives follow the arcs of biracial protagonists who pass within white society, a choice from which they both suffer psychologically and relationally. These books and others like them offer suggestive claims in their own rights about the importance of appreciating and serving a larger African American community. Even as such texts deconstruct "race" as a visual or biological signifier, they posit the significance of identifying with a shared racial history.

How did Harlem Renaissance artistic endeavors contribute to ideologies of racial uplift and debates over assimilation?

As we have been claiming across our various sites of inquiry, a discourse on race in relation to new modernism must take serious account of the problems embedded in any attempt to treat aesthetics and politics as separate scions of a larger modernist project. The Harlem Renaissance was characterized not only by fictional, poetic, and artistic representations of African American life but also by debates surrounding racial uplift and black political/ideological endeavors. Some of the main figures of the Renaissance—Alain Locke, W. E. B. Du Bois, Marcus Garvey—are some of the best-known and most anthologized thinkers in the latter domain. Each played a pivotal role in shaping African American political priorities in the early decades of the twentieth century. Their works were occupied by topics such as, among others, migration, segregation, authority, and experimentation—all foundational matters in discourses on modernism. The different paths they charted in the service of African American progressive political ideology were facilitated by important concepts like Locke's **New Negro**, which connected with Pound's admonition to "make it new." Crucially connected to the concept of newness was the notion of **authorship** and authority in the Harlem Renaissance, for what did it mean to be an African American author in the dawning of a new century following a history of contested relevance? Harlem Renaissance writers from Hurston to DuBois found one answer to that question in their depictions of the **folk**.

New Negro

For Hurston, an exploration and celebration of African American culture was a new and powerful idea in the evolution of Harlem writers. Though a character like Janie in *Their Eyes Were Watching*

God found herself indebted to traditions and histories that defined her identity, she simultaneously sought to break free from them and chart her own course. What did it mean to be "new" as an African American in a culture that saw you as primitive? We introduced the concept of Washington's vocational, accommodationist agenda with Tuskegee above, as well as Baker's positioning of Washington as a central figure—if not *the* originator—of what he labels Afromodernism. But it was the generation of black leaders after Washington who began to shape a twentieth-century discourse about the social, economic, and political realities and potentials for African Americans' in the United States, a conversation that remained central to the Harlem Renaissance. W. E. B. Du Bois's philosophical approach to the question of African Americans' rights in the new century was influenced heavily by his studies at Fisk and Harvard University and his embracing of the pragmatist writings of William James, of whom he became a friend and confidante. Hutchison argues that Du Bois "saw black culture, black labor, and racist oppression as far more central to American civilization than could the dominant pragmatists of the early twentieth century," and so, engaged with the philosophy (especially its whitewashing of civilization) to expand it (37). Du Bois's philosophical underpinnings represent both a rejection of Washington's insistence that vocation and economic enfranchisement are tantamount to black civilization's influence in America and the promotion of the belief that art must do political work to have any value.

In *Slaves to Fashion: Black Dandyism and the Styling of Black Diasporic Identity* (2009), Monica L. Miller nicely describes this knotty relationship between art and politics. She turns to "The Negro in Literature and Art" (1913), an essay in which Du Bois sets out "to formulate an aesthetic theory that takes advantage of his earlier argument and combats the perceived mutual exclusivity of the realms of politics and culture" (146):

> Hoping to articulate a way for a "group of radicals" to move beyond mere appreciation of art to a perception of its potential for embodying and wielding cultural and political power, [Du Bois] promotes art and beauty as constituent parts of the arsenal needed for the "pushing onward" or the continuation of the struggle for African American civil rights. (146)

Crystallizing a collapse of the ostensible aesthetics/politics binary, he would later write succinctly that he did not "care a damn for any art that is not used for propaganda" ("Criteria of Negro Art" 29).

Hutchinson notes that "Du Bois's chief antagonist as a philosopher and aesthetician was . . . Alain Locke . . . a more thoroughgoing cultural pluralist than Du Bois" (39). For Locke, art was a mediator that offered potential to articulate what he saw as some fundamental truths about African American lives in a way that propaganda could not. Hutchinson puts Locke with the "writers associated with the Harlem Renaissance, both black and white, [who] believed that realistic fiction, poetry, and drama would bring greater intellectual understanding by exploring the psychology of racism as well as opening a space for the re-creation and expression of diversely 'American' selves" (42). Echoing a conventional, if troubling, chronology, David Levering Lewis marks 1925 as "Year I of the Harlem Renaissance" in large part because of the publication of Locke's *The New Negro* (see *When Harlem*). The pivotal volume evolved both from a special issue on Harlem in the periodical *Survey Graphic* and from a literary contest sponsored by Charles S. Johnson, who was the editor of *Opportunity* at the time. *Opportunity*'s mission statement was to "depict Negro life as it is with no exaggerations. We shall try to set down interestingly but without sugar-coating or generalization the findings of careful scientific surveys and the facts gathered from research" (Ferguson 185). Unlike *The Crisis*, whose writers included James Weldon Johnson, W. E. B. Du Bois, and William Pickens, among others, *Opportunity* was situated as a literary magazine. For Johnson, the literary was one of the "aspects of the cultural side of Negro life that have been neglected" (Jones 188).

Early in 1925, Johnson created a literary contest for *Opportunity* that would be judged by distinguished artists and socialists. He described its purpose and goals as follows:

[The contest] hopes to stimulate and encourage creative literary effort among Negroes; to locate and orient Negro writers of ability; to stimulate and encourage interest in the serious development of a body of literature about Negro life, drawing deeply upon these tremendously rich sources; to encourage the reading of literature both by Negro authors and about Negro life, not merely because they are Negro authors but because what they write is literature and because literature is interesting, to foster a market for Negro writers and for literature by and about Negroes; to bring these writers into contact with the general world of letters to which they have been for the most part timid and inarticulate strangers; to stimulate and foster a type of writing by Negroes which shakes itself free of deliberate propaganda and protest! (Vol 2.21 [September 1924] 259)

The very announcement of the award echoed the ethos of Du Bois's involvement with *The Crisis*. In *Opportunity*, literature would not be a form of propaganda or a path to air grievances but would instead represent a way in which African Americans could describe their social realities in ways that would resonate with white audiences. A mission that directly involved the importance of a white audience would make Locke's blended anthology, comprising of pieces on Harlem in *Opportunity* which won awards and *Survey Graphic*, a highly contested work among black writers and intellectuals.

The resulting book signaled the beginning of something new for many critics and scholars of African American literature. While the phrase "new negro" had been in common usage for almost thirty years by the time Locke published his anthology, it is from the first section of *The New Negro* that the word "renaissance" is used to describe the writing of a so-called "Negro Renaissance." Beyond launching the careers of many authors who, in the words of Lewis, would become "future Harlem Renaissance regulars," *The New Negro* advocated a new path forward wherein descriptions of African American society more broadly would make a particular point appealing to white intellectuals and artists. Hutchinson argues, "The very image of Africanism so important to *The New Negro* is often mediated through white perceptions and artistic traditions . . . the experience of people of African descent in a country where that descent meant something very different from what it had ever meant in Africa itself" (399). It marked a turn from both "Garveyism and socialism" and toward "Phi Beta Kappa poets, university-trained painters, concertizing musicians, and novel-writing civil rights officials" (Lewis 118). This emphasis on cultural translation by way of artistic ideals aimed to provide a connective tissue that would link African American art and European aesthetics. As James F. Wilson puts it, Locke espoused a "utopian notion of a convergent black and white modernism" that would cultivate "a pluralist, universal art" (9).

Beyond offering a definition of "newness" or "rebirth," Locke thus attempted to craft in *The New Negro* a rhetoric for racial representation by way of a European model of modern aesthetics. Further, he was advocating a political agenda directly in contrast to the ones offered by Washington and Du Bois; Locke argued that, through art, one affirms that "the conditions that . . . mold . . . a New Negro are [also] molding a new American attitude" (*Works of Alain Locke* 447). Henry Louis Gates, Jr., writes in his essay "The Trope of a New Negro and the Reconstruction of the Image of the Black" that the kind of thinking espoused by Locke offered racial uplift through a kind of metonymic paradigm that presented representational and cultural aestheticism as a joint effort for both black and white Americans. Gates suggests that, for Locke, there was a "correlation between the specific *characteristics* of the individuals depicted and the larger *character* of the race" (13). Similarly, Miriam Thaggert concludes that Locke's philosophy was, simply, "better literature *by* blacks and better images *of* blacks in literature would positively affect the general, national perception of African Americans" (10).[4]

Going a bit further, Houston Baker argues that "*The New Negro*, like the valued documents from which we grasp iconic images and pictorial myths of a colonial or frontier America, is perhaps our first *national* book, offering not only a description of streams of tendency in our collective lives but also an actual construction within its pages of the sounds, songs, images, and signs of a nation" (*Modernism* 85). And yet, Baker is quick to note that Locke's anthology is not "the clearest instance of a full discursive engagement *with* such mass energies [of a nation]" (91). In his reading of *The New Negro*, Baker offers a distinctive binary between Renaissance/"renaissancism." The former is a descriptor employed by Locke and codified as representative of a singular endeavor, while the latter represents "a complete expressive modernity . . . achieved . . . [through] a *spirit* of nationalistic engagement that begins with intellectuals, artists, and spokespersons at the turn of the century and receives extensive definition and expression during the 1920s" (91; emphasis in original). By thinking about Locke and his anthology through this notion of "renaissancism," Baker claims we can better assess what role the Harlem Renaissance played in an evolution of modernism more broadly. We again confront the collapse of an aesthetics/politics dichotomy: a black artist first became aware in this context, Baker suggests, "that his or her only possible foundation for authentic and modern expressivity resides in a discursive field marked by formal mastery and sounding deformation" (91). Refashioning "Renaissance" as "renaissancism" also challenges scholars to avoid thinking of this context for African American modernist art as confined to one historical moment and instead think of it as a "productive set of tactics, strategies, and syllables that takes form at the turn of the century and extends to our own day" (91–92).

Authorship

In his 1895 poem "We Wear the Mask," poet Paul Laurence Dunbar writes,

We wear the mask that grins and lies,
It hides our cheeks and shades our eyes,—
This debt we pay to human guile;
With torn and bleeding hearts we smile,
And mouth with myriad subtleties.

The excerpt from the larger poem identifies one of the critical problems for African Americans in the early decades of the twentieth century as that of performing race before a white audience who was used to seeing African Americans largely in stereotypical and conventional tropes of the smiling and content enslaved worker on a plantation. As African American writers and artists grappled with their own relationships to various modernist themes—individualism and presumed subjective interiority among them—metaphors of masks and masking proliferated.

Du Bois suggests in his book *Souls of Black Folk* that being an African American in the turn of the century is to see one's experiences as if through a veil: "It dawned upon me with a certain suddenness that I was different from the others; or like [them perhaps] in heart and life and longing, but shut out from their world by a vast veil"

(2). Du Bois later claims that his metaphorical sense of a veil creates a two-ness of identity, bifurcating an interior world of self and an exterior world of race that threatens African Americans' very existences:

> It is a peculiar sensation, this double-consciousness, this sense of always looking at one's self through the eyes of others, of measuring one's soul by the tape of a world that looks on in amused contempt and pity. One ever feels his two-ness—an American, a Negro; two souls, two thoughts, two unreconciled strivings; two warring ideals in one dark body, whose dogged strength alone keeps it from being torn asunder. (3)

Dunbar's and Du Bois's formulations of veils, masks, and double consciousness also provide useful tropes in relation to the fraught notion of authorship during the Harlem Renaissance. If Locke's *The New Negro* offered literary and artistic modes as means by which to articulate a unifying cultural plurality, the project of producing art for an audience became a vastly more complicated concept. For Locke, the idea of African American art must include, perhaps first and foremost, an acknowledgment of audience and peers, white intellectuals and artists in whose company they wished to be included. The realities of patronage—in which, as discussed earlier, African American artists partnered with wealthy white socialites and intellectuals who supported their work—offered financial backing but implicitly prevented autonomous authorship in the process.

Dunbar's poetics are complicated for African American poets during the Harlem Renaissance not least because of his turn to "dialect." When he writes of wearing "the mask," then, we are reminded—as mentioned in our first section on the dialect of modernism—of the difficulties that renderings of an African American vernacular presented in relation to ideals of racial uplift. Black writers were expected to write in hackneyed over-exaggerations of a dialect with which white readers were comfortable—one that fueled stereotypes of African American naiveté and ignorance. In his essay "Dis and Dat: Dialect and Descent," Henry Louis Gates, Jr., rejects "the mask" as a suitable image of problems of authorship in relation to modern African American literature. Especially noting the problems of its presumed stasis, he suggests instead the model of the "mask in motion" in which there is no plane division between notions of interiority and exteriority. Based on African masks, the mask in motion "is a metaphor for dialectic—specifically, a dialectic or binary opposition embracing unresolved or potentially irresolvable social forms, notions of origins, or complex issues of value" (*Figures in Black* 168).[5]

Using Gates's concept of a "mask in motion" that collapses the supposed contradictions implied by an inside/outside dichotomy, we might begin to think more critically about ideas of "authorship," "authority," "authenticity," "fidelity," and other essentialist rhetorics that were deployed in different ways toward different ends during the Harlem Renaissance. Doing so would allow scholars to present a concept like authorship, for example, as inevitably servicing contradictory and competing modes of modernist aesthetics and politics. As Steven A. Nardi concludes in his essay on Laurence Dunbar and Countee Cullen, "the logic of modernism itself insists on rendering the black face unseen, a presence that both reveals itself and disappears in the same gesture" (132).

Langston Hughes and Zora Neale Hurston are two prominent figures of the Harlem Renaissance whose work is intimately connected with the notion of audience and patronage. Hurston even invented a word—"Negrotarians"—for "whites who specialized in Afro-American uplift" (Lewis 98). David Levering Lewis notes in *When Harlem Was in Vogue* that white investments in African American culture were not monolithic and singular. Many different socialites with different personal connections to literature and art found themselves caught up in the foment of art and writing that constituted the Harlem Renaissance:

> Some (Van Wyck Brooks, Hart Crane, Zona Gale, Waldo Frank) were drawn to Harlem on the way to Paris because it seemed to answer a need for personal nourishment and to confirm their vision of cultural salvation coming from the margins of civilization. Some expected the great renewal in the form of a political revolution and like [Claude] McKay's friends Muriel Draper, Louise Bryant, and Max Eastman, anticipated that the Afro-American would somehow play a major role in destroying the old order. (99)

Others, like Sherwood Anderson, were obsessed with the ostensible African American mind as the unlockable nexus to a mythos of creative terrain. He would write to the newspaper columnist H. L. Mencken, "Damn it, man, if I could really get inside the niggers and write about them with some intelligence, I'd be willing to be hanged later and perhaps would be" (99). In his lament to Mencken, one locates that same bifurcation of identity—the need to get *inside* that became crucial for white investment in what was deemed black culture.

One of the major patrons in the Harlem Renaissance, Carl Van Vechten, famously supported writers like Langston Hughes, Richard Wright, Ethel Waters, and Zora Neale Hurston but perhaps most infamously is known for his 1926 novel *Nigger Heaven*, which used Harlem as a setting for Van Vechten to explore his own obsession with "African American culture."[6] The publication of the novel became a flashpoint in the Renaissance for perhaps obvious reasons to do with Van Vechten's dubious claims to an accessible and authorial/ authoritative "insider status." James Smethurst argues in his book *The African American Roots of Modernism* (2011) that Van Vechten's book has much in common with "European modernists . . . with their well-known engagement with African art," in that it suggests that "white North American writers . . . need to get in touch with the vital currents of African American popular and folk cultures, must 'black up' a bit, in order to create a truly viable American modernism" (205). According to Smethurst, the novel ultimately fails not simply because of Van Vechten's authorial presumptions but because the book has a "total lack of historical context . . . [and] its characters are pure types without any capacity for transcending those types" (206).

As a result of the publication of *Nigger Heaven*, many authors of the Renaissance turned toward the notion of white patronage and investment in the literary and artistic aspirations of African Americans. A larger conversation began about what presumed responsibilities artists had to both their patrons and the white audiences for whom they wrote. Divisions among artists in the Harlem Renaissance over the expectations of authors and audiences had huge ramifications for figures like Richard Wright and Zora

Neale Hurston, the former taking Hurston to task for her seeming lack of "seriousness" in her fiction and the latter who refused Wright's ethos of protest as a genre of African American writing. In reviewing *Their Eyes Were Watching God* (1937) for the *New Masses*, Wright says of Hurston's novel:

> Miss Hurston can write, but her prose is cloaked in that facile sensuality that has dogged Negro expression since the days of Phillis Wheatley. Her dialogue manages to catch the psychological movements of the Negro folk-mind in their pure simplicity, but that's as far as it goes. Miss Hurston voluntarily continues in her novel the tradition which was forced upon the Negro in the theatre, that is, the minstrel technique that makes the "white folks" laugh. Her characters eat and laugh and cry and work and kill; they swing like a pendulum eternally in that safe and narrow orbit in which America likes to see the Negro live: between laughter and tears. . . . The sensory sweep of her novel carries no theme, no message, no thought. In the main, her novel is not addressed to the Negro, but to a white audience whose chauvinistic tastes she knows how to satisfy. She exploits that phase of Negro life which is "quaint," the phase which evokes a piteous smile on the lips of the "superior" race. (22–23)

Hurston would ultimately reject Wright's call for "motive fiction and social document fiction" by claiming to not "belong to [his] sobbing school of Negrohood who hold that nature somehow has given them a lowdown dirty deal and whose feelings are all but about it" ("How It Feels to Be a Colored Me" 1009). However, Wright's criticism of Hurston as a performer working on behalf of a white audience would be a critique leveled not just at her but other artists of the Renaissance, as well. Langston Hughes would write his classic essay "The Negro Artist and the Racial Mountain" for *The Nation* in 1926 attacking an unnamed poet—presumably Countee Cullen—for wanting to write in for/like white poets and not for/about/to his race: "I am ashamed for the black poet who says, 'I want to be a poet, not a Negro poet,' as though his own racial world were not as interesting as any other world. I am ashamed, too, for the colored artist who runs from the painting of Negro faces to the painting of sunsets after the manner of the academicians because he fears the strange unwhiteness of his own features" (694).

In the essay, Hughes rejects "this urge within the race toward whiteness, the desire to pour racial individuality into the mold of American standardization, and to be as little Negro and as much American as possible" (694). This stance marks something of a pivot, of course, from Locke's privileging of cultural pluralism as a means of articulating what he saw as African Americans' unique place within modernism itself. Moreover, Hughes's codification of the division as a "racial mountain" delineated Harlem Renaissance writers and their approaches to traditions, aesthetics, and structures handed down by European modernists. We might think of Gates's concept of "the mask in motion" in dialogue with Baker's concept of "renaissancism" in order to read Harlem Renaissance writers' understandings of authorship as a kind of self-conscious genre in itself. Works of art or literature in this mode embraced multivocal and contradictory aesthetics and simultaneously greeted head-on the limits of economic, intellectual, and artistic possibility within a system of white patronage system.

Folk

In *The Big Sea* (1940), Langston Hughes wrote the following about
the aspirations and ignorance embedded in the Harlem Renaissance:

> Some Harlemites thought the millennium had come. They thought
> the race problem had at last been solved through Art. . . . They
> were sure the New Negro would lead a new life from then on in
> the green pastures of tolerance created by Countee Cullen, Ethel
> Waters, Claude McKay, Duke Ellington, Bojangles, and Alain
> Locke. I don't know what made any Negroes think that—except
> that they were mostly intellectuals doing the thinking. The ordinary
> Negroes hadn't heard of the Harlem Renaissance. And if they had,
> it hadn't raised their wages any. (228)

This articulation of the division between "the ordinary Negroes" and
the "new Negroes" of the Harlem Renaissance offers scholars a critical
point to investigate the primacy of class in the works of the writers
we examine in the 1920s and 1930s. For while the impoverished and
lower-class African Americans were often the subject of the Harlem
Renaissance poets and novelists, the aspirations of these artists
were to do with consolidating a literati, a series of intellectuals—the
"talented tenth," as Du Bois would call them—who would speak about
the issues and political concerns of their race. Usually comprised
of what we might call the "second wave" of Renaissance writers,
these individuals "turned radically to the black folk tradition for
inspiration, unlike Du Bois and Locke, for example, who associated
it with a crude or primitive aesthetics in need of literary refinement"
(Konzett 71).

During the time of the Harlem Renaissance, there was an explosion of investment in the culture of the "folk"—the "ordinary Negroes," to borrow Hughes's words—as the presumably authentic iteration of an African American identity. Often, artists pursued their desires to speak *to* a universal "black experience" by speaking *about* poor (often rural) African Americans, even as those same artists wished also to be engaged in an enterprise that spoke *of* cultural pluralism. Thus the dialogue surrounding the "folk" in Harlem Renaissance art, in many cases, failed to take account of how dramatically class discrepancies between writers and their subject matter can shape intellectual and aesthetic production. Furthermore, it adopted a sort of self-serving voyeuristic intrigue over primitivism akin to that held by expatriate writers discussed in our first chapter.

Many of the very foundational texts to the Harlem Renaissance— Claude McKay's *Harlem Shadows* (1922), Langston Hughes's *The Weary Blues* (1926), Jean Toomer's *Cane* (1923), and Zora Neale Hurston's *Mules and Men* (1935), to give a few examples—offer the "folk" as emblematic of an authentic or authoritative African American perspective/voice. Writing about Toomer's "Fern" section in *Cane*, critic Barbary Foley argues in her *Jean Toomer: Race, Repression, and Revolution* that Toomer uses the trope of "folk" for a whole host of thematic concerns: "Women with the folk, the folk with the soil, and the soil with the region; the ideologeme of metonymic nationalism patently guides the narrator's retrospective representation of the story's title character" (206). However, instead of offering truths about "folk" in Georgia, the text of "Fern" instead centers on the breaking of the narrator's expectations about what such poor people are and how they operate. Foley notes that "Fern" gradually becomes a narrative not about the woman the narrator observes but about the way in which his bad reading of her causes confusion for both the reader and the narrator. He cannot, for example, understand the song she sings because "it does not conform to his expectations of folk authenticity" (207).

When Toomer leaves Fern where she is, instead of having her escape her rootedness in the Georgia sun, Foley argues that it is a celebration of his artistic and urban privilege. In his closing section, the narrator asserts, "Better that she listen to folk-songs by dusk in Georgia, you would say, and so would I," a statement that Foley finds indicative of the problem of using the folk as a symbol for any kind of modernist artistic project:

> The ease with which he proposes that Fern is best left where she is—what business would she have in a Harlem tenement, or even married to a northern doctor or lawyer?—testifies, moreover, to [the narrator's] writerly investment in viewing this woman as an embodiment of the Georgia soil. . . . He does not want her to become part of the project of modernity that northward migration would entail; he is comfortable with—indeed, comforted by—her position, geographical, historical, and symbolic in the rural dusk. Sufficiently cosmopolitan to valorize Fern's hybridity, the narrator cannot imagine she might herself participate in the formation of a cosmopolitan future. (208)

Foley's argument is useful here in examining other Renaissance artists' deployments of "folk" rhetoric and typology in the service of their own modernist projects. In this vein, Toomer's narrator fetishizes her image and comes to embody "the complicity of the

North in the continuing subjugation of the South; of art in acceding to an oppressive social order" (209).

In complicating the notion of accurately representing "the folk," then, we find in Harlem Renaissance writings a similar anxiety about representations of migrations from rural spaces (presented as metonymic sites for poverty) to the urban oases of big cities (offered as sites connoting wealth, prosperity, and community). As noted earlier in this chapter, the idea of Harlem as a nexus of the artistic and the cultural was facilitated in large part because of the "Great Migration" of African Americans during Reconstruction. The migration of African Americans from a largely rural South to major northern cities contributed to a narrative of urban-based uplift, whereby African Americans could forge a new sense of racial community. Smethurst notes the significance of this transition: "The African American community nationwide, which was still very rural in the 1890s became predominantly urban by the 1940s. . . . In short, this migration was enormous" (97).

And yet, Smethurst notes that "migration narratives" by Harlem Renaissance writers are not, on the whole, celebratory; in fact, he finds in many of them a "sense of melancholy" as "the black subject is caught up in an impossible existential bind in the United States" (121). The black "folk" of the South who travel North to the urban centers that promise them freedom find instead the "urban ghetto," a site that is "simultaneously [a] new home, refuge, trap, and exile, of black metropolis and destroyer of black culture and racial values" (121) While finding these narratives resisting the trajectory established by earlier forms of African American writing such as slave narratives, Smethurst does locate in them a kinship with "a certain modernist sensibility in U.S. and European fiction" in that characters find themselves "radically divided intellectually. The sort of radical alienation and fragmentation that will come to be associated with artistic modernism is here writ large" (122). This makes sense, then, of Zora Neale Hurston's emphasis on what Eve E. Dunbar calls "non-northern black life" (170).[7] Such an emphasis was emblematic of both Harlem Renaissance and broader modernist projects, for it contests dominant notions that "insisted that black modernity and progress was commensurate with migration to northern metropolises" (170). Instead, Hurston is at pains to offer the folk—a figure she carefully studied for the majority of her life[8]—as a complicated trope that "requires that we think differently about how we constitute the relationship between 'black modernity' and 'black folk' . . . [by] a revised but affirmed possibility for black national belonging . . . carried out through the ethnographic form" (Dunbar 17).

In this sense, Hurston is not alone in her ethnographic interest in African American "folk culture." Indeed, the very title of Du Bois's famous 1903 sociological treatise on African American life invokes the figure of fascination for Hurston: *The Souls of Black Folk*. Du Bois organizes his fourteenth chapter around an interrogation of the values of what he calls "The Sorrow Songs." These songs—which Du Bois reads as both a literary analysis and an ethnographic study— offer for America the first articulation of a distinctly nationalistic and, he argues, modern voice:

> What are these songs, and what do they mean? I know little of music and can say nothing in technical phrase, but I know something of men, and knowing them, I know that these songs are the articulate

message of the slave to the world. . . . They are the music of an unhappy people, of the children of disappointment; they tell of death and suffering and unvoiced longing toward a truer world, of misty wanderings and hidden ways. The songs are indeed the siftings of centuries; the music is far more ancient than the words, and in it we can trace here and there signs of development. . . . This was primitive African music. (538)

In connecting the vernacular of his forefathers to the language of his father, Du Bois offers the folk song as a tradition of modernity that predates European modernity itself ("Before the Pilgrims landed we were here. Here we have brought our three gifts and mingled them with yours: a gift of story and song," he argues in the text [538]). Du Bois's celebration of the "sorrow song," and its complicated articulation of sadness and hope, of course, evokes another African American artistic genre in Harlem at the time: the blues.

Houston Baker's formative project *Modernism and the Harlem Renaissance* (1987), which, as previously noted, helped pave the way for studies of African American modernism, was published just three years after his groundbreaking *Blues, Ideology, and Afro-American Literature: A Vernacular Theory* (1984). In that earlier book, Baker offers the blues not simply as an object of study but as an analytical framework to discuss the class-conscious ideological underpinnings of what he calls a "blues voice." This significant analytical arc establishes the blues as a key element in and outgrowth of African American modernism. Another foundational scholar of the Harlem Renaissance and black modernist thought, Arnold Rampersad, talks about blues as a modernist aesthetic as well.[9] Employing his work in a discussion of Langston Hughes, Jahan Ramazani discusses the crucial relationship between blues and modernism in *Poetry of Mourning* (1994):

> Hughes found in the blues, Arnold Rampersad argues, "the tone, the texture, the basic language of true black modernism": whereas Wheatley adapts the Neoclassical elegy and Cullen the Romantic elegy, Hughes adapts the stark, ironic, and melancholic form of the blues, creating an indigenous literary equivalent to the modern elegy. (138)

His description of the blues as "indigenous" is worth considering here, along with his claim that Hughes's blues poems offered "distinctly African-American genre of melancholic mourning" (138). Certainly, the case is that the blues served as a crucible for black suffering, American politics, aesthetic craft, and modernist innovation. Taking the complexity of this nexus seriously, however, demands a critical reckoning with ideas about distinctness and indigeneity. New modernist scholarly turns challenge the notion of race and experience as *things* that can have inherent or distinct qualities that characterize them ontologically. Indeed, blues aesthetics and thematics (and, of course, those of its jazz corollary) showcase the contingencies of racial identifications, the arbitrariness of perimeters that would bound them.

In their lives and their work—their politics and their aesthetics— blues icons Ma Rainey and Bessie Smith are cases in point. Both born in the Deep South, Rainey and Smith enjoyed the height of their careers in Harlem. Their songs included conventional blues themes that paired social subjugation with personal longing, but they also dealt overtly with queerness, gender roles, and lesbian sexual desire.

Ma Rainey's "Prove It on Me" is a good example, wherein Rainey talks about wearing "a collar and a tie" and going out with friends who "must've been women, 'cause I don't like no men."[10] The incorporation of queer desire in traditional blues forms presented consumers with multiple marginalizations, disallowing a straightforward reading of a singular "black experience."

Thinking outward

The bustling music scene in Harlem brought complex systems of exchange—between performers and audiences, buyers and sellers, marketers and consumers—into stark relief. The whites-only Cotton Club, which featured popular black musicians in Prohibition-era Harlem, was a hotbed of these dynamics. Deemed "a Jim Crow Club for gangsters and monied whites" by Langston Hughes,[11] the nightclub provided white patrons with a glitzy form of black spectacle. In this way, it offered a brand of exotic pastiche to eager white consumers who enjoyed being entertained by black performers (Bessie Smith among them) without having to interact with them. The lines between production and consumption, of course, echo the difficulties discussed earlier in this chapter with pinning down a discrete notion of unmediated authorship. In obvious ways, of course, the distance between the black performer and the white audience member at a segregated club—a chasm wherein the effects of racial prejudice play out quite literally on stage—could not be greater. In other ways that were just as significant but much more nuanced, however, black and white people alike were caught up in economic systems managing performance, purchase, and profit. One need only look to the fact that the owner of the Cotton Club—a British-immigrant-turned-New York-mobster-and-bootlegger Owney Madden—bought the nightspot from none other than extravagant black boxer Jack Johnson, retaining Johnson as manager.

In our next chapter, then, we look at some of these more nebulous configurations of authorship and audience that posited celebrity and racial otherness as two sides of the same coin. These dynamics took shape in domains like music, dance, and theater, but they also appeared in sports as black athletes began using their own celebrity status to challenge expectations and assumptions of racial performance. These popular stages and those who performed on them showcase the ways in which cumbersome but calculated economic machines obscured even as they manufactured racial and modernist formulations.

Notes

1 See his review in *New Masses*, October 5 (1937): 22–23.

2 See his review "Recent Negro Fiction" in *New Masses*, August 5 (1940): 22–26.

3 There has been a wealth of scholarship in recent decades that discuss the ways in which classification systems invent and deploy definitions of "race" with devastating and far-reaching consequences for those to whom they are applied. Two of particular note are Stephanie Smallwood's *Saltwater Slavery: A Middle Passage from Africa to American Diaspora* (Harvard UP, 2008), which talks about colonial-era taxonomies that turned captives into capital; and Colin Dayan's *The Law Is a White Dog: How Legal Rituals Make and Unmake Persons* (Princeton UP, 2013), which brings the discussion into contemporary modes of jurisprudence.

4 See *Images of Black Modernism: Verbal and Visual Strategies of the Harlem Renaissance* (U of Massachusetts P, 2010).

5 See also Baker's concluding essay "Why the Lega Mask Has Many Mouths and Multiple Eyes," in *The Trouble with Post-Blackness*, Houston A. Baker, Jr. and K. Merinda Simmons, eds. (New York: Columbia UP, 2015).

6 Of the prominent patrons of that context, Van Vechten looms largest through the artistic legacy of, among other things, his famous photographic portraits of Harlem Renaissance figures. He was also the literary executor for Gertrude Stein.

7 See *Black Regions of the Imagination: African American Writers Between the Nation and the World* (2013).

8 From *Mules and Men* (1935) to *Tell My Horse* (1938) to the posthumously and recently published *Barracoon: The Story of the Last "Black Cargo"* (2018), Hurston's anthropological interest in folklore maintains a strong presence throughout her work.

9 Rampersad's earliest books established him as a leading figure in early studies of the Harlem Renaissance. See *The Art and Imagination of W.E.B. Du Bois* (Harvard, 1976) and the two-volume *The Life of Langston Hughes* (Oxford, 1986, 1988).

10 Bessie Smith and Ma Rainey were, of course, only two women among many performers—Ethel Waters and Josephine Baker among them—who had sexual relationships with other women. In 1925, Ma Rainey was arrested in Harlem for holding a sex party for women at her home. She was bailed out the next morning by none other than Bessie Smith.

11 See Tricia Welsch, "Killing Them with Tap Shoes." *Journal of Popular Film & Television*. 25.4 (1998).

5

Selling Otherness: Racial Performance and Modernist Marketing

The 1942 photograph used as cover image for this book is of singer, actor, and activist Paul Robeson leading Oakland shipyard workers in singing the national anthem. Seven years later, Robeson would be effectively blacklisted after giving a speech in Paris that was portrayed in US media as having expressed solidarity among black Americans with the Soviet Union. A year after that, in 1950, the US government revoked his passport, and he was barred from traveling abroad for nearly a decade. An outspoken critic of American domestic and foreign policies that maintained racial and economic disparity, Robeson was formally questioned about his communist sympathies, and he was the subject of investigations by various government agencies, including the FBI and CIA. In a particularly conspiratorial moment, the House Un-American Activities Committee questioned a reluctant Jackie Robinson, compelling him to critique Robeson's Paris speech. The photograph of Robeson with the shipyard workers is striking in a number of ways, evocatively demonstrating the economic framework for his race politics. Workers' rights were civil rights and vice versa, a claim Robeson announced from his platform as a pop culture icon.

We have claimed throughout this volume that, far from resting in distinct spheres, ideas of "race" and "modernism" are formed in and through one another. The constitutive work of each term is evident across a host of geospatial and sociopolitical contexts, exhibited in every case through various modes of literary and artistic performance. In our final chapter, we will look at physical performances by and of people of color—on stages, in front of microphones, and in baseball fields and boxing rings. These art forms that brought the body front and center were fueled by the political and economic underpinnings of modernist ideology and, as such, were sites of both exploitation and resistance. Of particular interest to us are the methods and strategies for marketing and consuming racial otherness. But first, we should spend some time with the concept of "performance" as it has figured into race and identity studies over the past few decades. Its rhetorical evolutions and theoretical implications in these scholarly discussions have been vital for new modernism and the field's productive challenges to the idea of a stable modernist canon.

Often in discussions of performance, especially when emphasizing racial dynamics therein, a quickly invoked concept is that of "cultural expression" or "expressive style/form." Brenda

Dixon Gottschild, for example, suggests, "Those who read and write about it today need to regard minstrelsy as, on the one hand, a white conceit having little to do with African American anything and, on the other hand, a genre that expropriated and imitated bona fide Africanist expressive forms" (1996, 83), while Tyler Stovall notes "the role of expressive culture in the creation of community solidarities and traditions" (1996, 222).

Further, in *Staging Race: Black Performers in Turn of the Century America* (2006), Karen Sotiropoulos discusses the multiplicity and playfulness with which black performers approached language and self-presentation, but she describes the improvisation and wit embedded in these modes of art as follows: "Hardly intended to be direct representations, their expressive cultures were enactments of their feelings, thoughts, and imaginations" (242). This is understandable enough. When talking about the performing arts, this rhetoric of expressivity serves as a shorthand signifier for the influences of history, experience, politics, and context that are brought to bear before an audience (or, in the case of sports, as will also be discussed in this chapter, a group of spectators). What this nomenclature relies upon, however, is an implicit realm of interiority—"feelings, thoughts, and imaginations" held inside and subsequently expressed outward. An examination of modernist performances, however, quickly reveals "race" to be an idea consolidated through those very performances. Pressing this shift—from descriptive accounts of performances to analytical accounts of performativity (a distinction which will be discussed further below)—is one of the ways in which a new modernist turn intervenes and provides space for more nuanced discussions about the power dynamics at work in identifications and stagings of race.

As Kobena Mercer suggests in a very succinct and useful subtitle to her essay "Diaspora Aesthetics and Visual Culture," "Modernism was always multicultural."[1]

Critical queries

How and why do physical performances serve as a metonym for modernity writ large?

When thinking about modernism, particular images stand out, like Josephine Baker's iconic skirt of bananas. What sets apart these performance-based images (specifically in this chapter, in relation to music, dance/theater, and sports) and gives them status as a metonym for modernity more broadly? We have been talking at length about the ways in which aesthetics were a conduit for political statements and mobilizations and vice versa. As Benjamin Brawley announced in *The Negro in Literature and Art in the United States* (1918), "if in connection with [art] we study the Negro we shall find that two things are observable. One is that any distinction so far won by a member of the race in America has been almost always in some one of the arts; and the other is that any influence so far exerted by the Negro on American civilization has been primarily in the field of aesthetics" (4). So how did this perceived connection between black life and artistic form take shape in contexts that put artists/performers in the same room with their audiences? In what ways were visual signifiers of race manufactured, marketed, and consumed as a key element in those performances? We will focus on two features in particular: (1) the role of performance in creating the very notion of the icons (Josephine Baker, Billie Holiday, Jesse Owens, etc.) we recognize as such and (2) the advertising methods and strategies in the modernist era that created and subsequently stoked spectator desire.

How did a semblance of race come to be consolidated through performances of racial stereotypes?

It has become easy enough to talk about "race" as a social construction, but modernist musical/theater/athletic performances provide contexts that allow us to see this in action. Modernist identifications of race were formed and reinforced through rhetoric, mimicry, and business models. In this way, the very notion of race itself was a product that could be bought and sold. A helpful theoretical tool in thinking of race in this manner is the concept of performativity. Far from "race" being a stable or self-evident thing in the world, it is rather a complex and operationalized system of acts of identification (to use to Jean-François Bayart's terminology), the impression of which is consolidated through repeated performances of certain social scripts and expectations. That is not at all to suggest a kind of amorphous universalism that denies the existence of race. Indeed, the *effects* of these social scripts being played out again and again are matters of life and death, and the stakes of these scripts could not be higher. The popularity of minstrel performances is a prime example. Racial stereotypes played out on stages, entertaining large audiences. White actors in blackface fueled racist ideas of black inferiority through their performances, consequently perpetuating and justifying the lower social status occupied by people of color.

How did modernist markets function, at once offering "race" as a profit generator and presenting Europe as an ideal of escape and cosmopolitanism for black Americans?

In post-Reconstruction America, performance venues and opportunities for people of color reflected in many ways their broader societal realities. Clubs were segregated, and black performers were often forbidden from interacting with their white audiences. Marketing strategies that promoted performers of color often used race as a central advertising feature, packaging an exotic other that spectators happily consumed. In this context, European city centers like London and Paris emerged as symbols of escape from provincial American racism, and African American performers—modernist ex-patriots in their own rights—found career success and made new lives across the Atlantic Ocean. One of the most famous and certainly most iconic figures in this cohort was Josephine Baker, who began her career as a Harlem Renaissance vaudeville chorus girl and who became a French sensation as audiences grew more fascinated with primitivism and African art forms (Baker posed for Picasso as well). There should not be presumed, however, a stark distinction between American discrimination and European embrace of a racial otherness fantasy. Indeed, Brent Hayes Edwards begins *The Practice of Diaspora* by observing that W. E. B. Du Bois's famous claim that "the problem of the twentieth century is the problem of the color line," predates *The Souls of Black Folk* where it later appeared in print. It was, in fact, part of a speech Du Bois gave in London at the Pan-African Conference in 1900 (1). Thus, the problem he presented was an international rather than an exclusively American one.

In what ways did artistic and athletic performances serve as sites of resistance and/or political activism?

Celebrity status provided a space of slippage in traditional codifications of racial otherness that gave performers of color chances to deviate from and revise those very codes. Particularly of interest to us in this chapter is how black celebrities used their social and economic capital to confront racist ideas, policies, and systems. The means and methods by which they did so varied, of course. In some cases, black performers refused to appear at whites-only venues or sang protest songs (Billie Holiday's "Strange Fruit" added lynching to the topics of jazz and blues standards). In other cases, they refused to comply with respectability politics that came from within black communities (Josephine Baker brought erotic dancing into high society, and Jack Johnson wore fur coats and had relationships with white women). Whatever the method and whatever their performance genre, these variations and revisions combated the idea of a monolithic or authentic "black culture."

Performativity is a key concept in these challenges to a stable notion of culture or identity, as it helps make a shift from thinking about a social actor outside a performance to thinking about the ways in which social performances consolidate and perpetuate a semblance of a self or subject who would "act" in the first place. Our discussion will then take up the interplay between **mimicry and minstrelsy**, both of which were vital integers in the marketing, selling, and consumption of racial difference. These modes of performing and, by extension, reifying ideas about otherness were partnered with both progressivism and orientalism in international contexts, so we will spend some time on **transnationalism** and **marketing** before turning to the ways performers used their celebrity status to advance their particular brands of racial **activism**.

Performance and performativity

For the purposes of this chapter, we are going to think about "performance" in broad terms, so as to place athletes alongside opera singers and vaudeville actors. Important in this rendering are the roles of marketing and consuming physical performances that happen before spectators. When we think about performance, there are typically a few things mentally up and running, not least of which is the idea of the person behind the presentation. Outside the costume, away from the microphone, beneath the sports uniform is the *real* Josephine Baker or Billie Holiday or Jack Johnson, whose "behind-the-legend"-esque biographies offer no end in entertaining pop documentary fodder. Another tempting way to talk about performances as being rooted in the real is to suggest, as many scholars have done, that performances by black people are manifestations of an underlying African consciousness or set of traditions. Examples of this approach can be found in Gale Jackson's "The Way We Do: A Preliminary Investigation of the African Roots of African American Performance" and Gerald L. Davis's *I Got the Word in Me and I Can Sing It, You Know: A Study of the Performed African-American Sermon*, just to name a couple. As we aim to show in this discussion, however, performance in the modernist era was integral in consolidating particular conceptions of race, as well as in providing spaces for subverting those conceptions.

Attending to the power dynamics that stacked up and shut down certain identifications of race to suit white markets means considering exactly how complicated the position—and, indeed, the very manufacturing—of a performer became in the modernist era. In this way, our discussion is more one of performativity than one of performance—a distinction that is worth emphasizing here inasmuch as it provides a new modernist rendering of canonical modernist physical texts.

The concept of performativity is most commonly associated with feminist philosopher and queer theorist Judith Butler, who popularized the term with her groundbreaking books *Gender Trouble* (1990) and *Bodies That Matter* (1993). To put it succinctly, while "performance" implies donning a role that expresses identity from the inside out, "performativity" suggests that actions and behaviors impart over time an *impression* of identity. Thus, identity is not a preexisting condition but is instead, according to this approach, the result of a series of performances, their repetitions and social effects. Butler explains with a useful summary in "Imitation and Gender Insubordination":

And if the "I" is the effect of a certain repetition, one which produces the semblance of a continuity or coherence, then there is no "I" that precedes the gender it is said to perform; the repetition, and the failure to repeat, produce a string of performances that constitute and contest the coherence of that "I." (311)

Importantly, the repetitions that create a sense of identity also present, Butler suggests, gaps that allow for disruption and revision: "Paradoxically, it is precisely the *repetition* of that play that establishes as well the *instability* of the very category that it constitutes" (311). With its contingency and precariousness exposed, "identity" is left open to new performances that have the potential to change its boundaries and registers. In other words, "if the 'I' is a site of repetition, that is, if the 'I' only achieves the semblance of identity through a certain repetition of itself, then the I is always displaced by the very repetition that sustains it" (311). This is borne out by various performances of "blackness"— the contexts and dimensions of which change as the category is identified, exaggerated, and/or nuanced. Partnering discourses on performativity in philosophy and theater or performance studies, Andrew Parker and Eve Kosofsky Sedgwick offer insightful analysis of "the relation of *speech* to *act*" and of "the relation of *act* to *identity*" (229). As they note, "a variety of critiques of agency . . . have begun to put interpretive pressure on the relations between the individual and the group as those are embodied, negotiated, or even ruptured by potent acts of speech or silence" (229). Performances in the modernist era quickly showed how such relations, quite literally play out.

Mimicry and minstrelsy

With her analysis of the white, famed songstress and Broadway performer Libby Holman (who enjoyed a great deal of fame in the 1920s–1930s New York), Jeanne Scheper offers an instructive example of the ways in which ideations of race were consolidated through performances. In *Moving Performances: Divas, Iconicity, and*

Remembering the Modern Stage (2016), Scheper discusses Holman's attempt to stage a particular mode of racial identification:

> In radio interviews, she made clear that the staging of her material went beyond a desire to disseminate or mimic African American art forms. For Holman, singing and performing produced what she imagined as a space of "becoming black." That is, she imagined what she performed as exceeding theatrical performance, as something more akin to the *performative* as used in the field of performance studies, where words carry the power to *do* something—what Jacques Derrida and Judith Butler, building on the British language philosopher J. L. Austin's 1955 Harvard speeches, understand as "the ways in which identities are constructed iteratively through complex citational processes." The performative utterance refers to that instance, as in an oath, when the force of repetition over time grants power, and "saying something," or singing something in Holman's case, is "doing" something. (99)

Her imagined figurative blackness marked Holman's attempt to have "distance from associations with historical genealogies that might locate her oeuvre in closer proximity to blackface performance and the reception traditions of minstrelsy, as well as from the torch song itself as emblematic of an era of marketing African American blues sound and performance traditions for white audiences through white bodies" (98). Of course, the efficacy of such an attempt relies upon its market—who buys and sells that particular mode of performance, how successful it is deemed.

The tension between becoming, mimicking, and masking is an important one to explore. After all, so much to do with racialized performances in the first few decades of the twentieth century had relied upon minstrel shows, wherein audiences bore witness to hackneyed racial stereotypes performed on stage by white actors. Using performance studies and cultural criticism as methodological points of entrée, Gottschild discusses Africanist presences in modes of performance—particularly dance. Borrowing her take on "Africanisms" from Joseph Holloway's *Africanisms in American Culture* (1990) and Toni Morrison's *Playing in the Dark* (1992), Gottschild similarly attends to the black themes, tropes, and presences on which white (and/or, those deemed neutrally "American") performances and aesthetic consumptions rely. Perhaps the most overt and obvious example of such reliance is the popularity of minstrel performances. Reaching their pinnacle in the 1830s and 1840s, minstrel shows lasted into the first decade of the twentieth century, until overtaken by vaudeville, which by that time had become the more ubiquitous mode of live comedic and musical performance in popular variety theater.

In a free association regarding the intersection of race, music, and modernism, the "Jazz Age" of the 1920s is a quick and representative standout. It can be easy to think simply of flappers and smoky Parisian cafés. But if we mark the beginning of modernism as Houston Baker does, with Booker T. Washington's 1895 Atlanta Exposition address, we might mark 1896 as a significant-albeit-dubious moment in modernist efforts toward African American self-determination. That was the year when the musical comedy *The Gold Bug* saw the addition of two black vaudeville performers: Bert Williams and George Walker. While headlining for the show, they popularized the "cakewalk"—a dance with plantation origins wherein enslaved people performed what became known as the cakewalk in way of mocking the formality of white entertainment. The dance then made regular appearances in minstrel shows, an irony which Amiri Baraka (publishing at the time as LeRoi Jones) notes with characteristic wit in his 1963 book *Blues People: Negro Music in White America*:

> If the cakewalk is a Negro dance caricaturing certain white customs, what is that dance, when, say, a white theater company attempts to satirize it as a Negro dance? I find the idea of white minstrels in blackface satirizing a dance satirizing a dance satirizing themselves a remarkable kind of irony—which, I suppose, is the whole point of minstrel shows. (86)

The layers of performance, mimicry, authorship, and identification here are emblematic of the ways in which modernist aesthetic projects and racial ideologies collapsed in on each other, never existing in separate spheres. The theoretical language of performativity that gained traction (in the way it continues to be used today) through Judith Butler's work in the 1990s—the decade that also began to shape the discourse of new modernism—helps describe this convergence and the resulting sociopolitical realities of the roles performed.

Williams and Walker troubled boundaries of mimicry and authenticity themselves as black men performing in burnt-cork blackface. Billing themselves as "Two Real Coons," they used racist rhetoric as an advertising device to set their show apart from those of much more prevalent white minstrels. In *Introducing Bert Williams: Burnt Cork, Broadway, and the Story of America's First Black Star*

(2008), Camille F. Forbes suggests that Williams and Walker "called into question the possible realness of blackface performers who only *emphasized* their artificiality by recourse to burnt cork" (59). Butler again proves useful here in her discussion of drag as a practice whose overperformance demonstrates the artifice of the ideal itself:

> Drag constitutes the mundane way in which genders are appropriated, theatricalized, worn, and done; it implies that all gendering is a kind of impersonation and approximation. If this is true, it seems, there is no original or primary gender that drag imitates, but *gender is a kind of imitation for which there is no original*; in fact, it is a kind of imitation that produces the very notion of the original as an *effect* and consequence of the imitation itself. (313)

It should be noted that minstrel performers occasionally sported feminine dress as well. Edward Le Roy Rice's 1911 cataloguing of *Monarchs of Minstrelsy, from "Daddy" Rice to Date* included two lists of "Famed Favorites Who Featured Feminine Fancies" (p. 201 and 241).[2] Of course, the politics and implications of these two very different sites of imitative performance should, however, not be conflated. Drag has long been a progressive site allowing for deviation from traditional gender norms, while blackface was a site that attempted to reinforce the norms of racist caricature. The point here is not to suggest the performances share something fundamental but rather to show that any imitation demonstrates the contingency of the category it performs.

Around the same time—in 1895—John William Isham, a white impresario of vaudeville theater, formed *Isham's Octaroons*. Coming off the heels of his work with the *Creole Burlesque Show*, which ended its run in 1897 and has been called the first black burlesque, Isham's new troupe featured black chorus girls. In this way, Isham relied upon traditional minstrel shows even as he departed from them. In 1896, Isham opened *Oriental America* with an exclusively African American cast on Broadway. The complicated dimensions of racial performance were also on display, though to a very different effect, as black performers employed white musical genres and contexts in their own work. Black performers like Billie Holiday, for example, reframed Tin Pan Alley songs in specifically African American contexts, utterly altering their connotations and resonances. Kobena Mercer suggests in her emphasis on the always-already multiculturalism of modernity that "as a site of cross-cultural interaction that created the soundtrack to twentieth-century modernity, from ragtime, blues, and jazz to rock and hip-hop, music bears witness to the deep inter-involvement of African Americans and European Americans in creating uniquely modernist forms" (154). In *Digging the Africanist Presence in American Performance: Dance and Other Contexts* (1996), Gottschild quotes from Nathan Irvin Huggins's *Harlem Renaissance* (1971) to provide an epigraph for a chapter taking up the politics and power dynamics present in minstrel performances: "The theatrical stage itself, more than any other cultural phenomenon, opens a perspective into the pathology of American race relations. It exposes the white-black dependence which has defined race relations in the United States and which persists despite all reform" (qtd. in Gottschild 245). If Huggins is right, such exposure surely accounts in part for the ways in which physical performance continue to serve as a metonym for modernity writ large.

Transnationalism

Alain Locke suggested in *The New Negro* that "in the very process of being transplanted, the Negro is becoming *transformed*" (113, emphasis in original). Speaking already in 1925 toward the concept we now call "performativity," Locke registers not simply a connection between but in fact a collapse of the utterance/occurrence and the person to whom it belongs or happens. There are many forms "being transplanted" took in the modernist era, of course, where we can see this process in action.[3] Monica L. Miller's *Slaves to Fashion*, for example, offers the image of the black dandy: "A concentration on the dandy's cosmopolitanism establishes the black dandy as a figure with both European and African and American origins, a figure who expresses with his performative body and dress the fact that modern identity, in both black and white, is necessarily syncretic, or mulatto, but in a liberating rather than constraining way" (178). Recognizing this liberating potential for a hybrid presentation of self, many African American performers left the United States for European city centers—Paris chief among them.

The First World War signaled a new level of exposure in France to American people, culture, and art forms. And while France maintained a colonial presence in Africa, the country represented a refuge of sorts for black Americans who faced endemic racism in the United States. In *Making Jazz French: Music and Modern Life in Interwar Paris* (2003), Jeffrey Jackson notes that French audiences had already been consumers of minstrel songs, cakewalks, and ragtime. But with the military orchestra of James Reese Europe, jazz began what would become its incredible foothold in the country (17).[4] French performers quickly adopted the unique sound that they associated with black American culture. As Jackson describes, the migrations of the music itself were not simply from the United States to Europe (specifically France). Jazz had not long before taken shape in the blending of musical styles in New Orleans, many of its key performers traveling north to larger, urban cities. Invoking Jelly Roll Morton, Sidney Bechet, King Oliver, and Louis Armstrong, all of whom left New Orleans within the first two decades of the twentieth century, Jackson brings into his discussion the interactions of performers and the various markets to which they brought their music: "Adapting jazz to different audiences was a critical element of the art from the beginning. Part of this adaptation, however, centered less on the musical than the racial component" (22). "Jazz Age Paris," then, as Tyler Stovall suggests, "represented an extreme example of both black community and black spectacle, therefore casting an interesting and instructive light on the interrelationship of the two" (222).

Josephine Baker has long served as a central figure for the intersection of community and spectacle in the Parisian creative scene. This status is due in part to her representing for French audiences a figure who could be at once exotic and close to home, a symbol of the Black Atlantic and an outgrowth of the fact that, as Jackson states, "jazz music became one of the first popular musics with a claim to being worldwide in scope" (23). The consumption of *l'art nègre* demonstrates the powerful way in which consuming something called "black culture" in fact *constructs* it. This is evident in the emphasis on the part of white audiences and music/art critics on African origins, perpetuating a fascination with the "exotic other" that they saw literally playing out on stage. Jackson describes this phenomenon as follows: "Labeling events that far predated the music of the 1920s with the term jazz simply because they depicted black musicians demonstrated a notion that jazz was a racial expression. It also revealed just how deeply many people believed the black roots of jazz could be traced. Jazz was somehow ancient, and its black essence was present long before the 1920s, many writers suggested" (26).

The orientalist popularity (and, by extension, profitability) of a presumed access to something ancient came by way of white performers as well, bringing the exotic with them to familiar, safer stages and allowing audiences to enjoy a voyeuristic relationship to racial otherness. In a discussion of modern dancer and innovator Loïe Fuller, who also spent the height of her career in Paris, Jeanne Scheper talks about the role of what she calls "racial drag":

> Racial drag is used as a tool to provide imagined access to this mineable orientalist archive of affectivity, and, in this era particularly, this orientalism is mined to produce a new, modern gendered subjectivity for the white performer. What is lost in the annals of dance and performance of this era is a full account of the ground upon which this repertoire was built. (92)

"This racial semiotics," Scheper suggests, "both produces distance from the anachronistically framed other and also builds on that different to innovate new modernisms" (92). Innovation, of course, was a key ingredient in identifying and presenting the avant-garde—a pivotal component of modernist performance that challenged mainstream conventions and mass production.[5] In contradistinction to "kitsch," which was seen as being profit driven and ripping off vanguard culture, the modernist impulses toward the avant-garde were steeped simultaneously in claims toward both newness and authenticity.

Marketing

Transatlantic markets drove the importing and exporting of modernist conceptions of race, primitivism, and cosmopolitanism. Simultaneously, of course, those processes of importing and exporting created those very markets. Before the critical turn to new modernism and its attendant emphasis on identity theory, scholarship coming out of the early 1980s looked at, among other things, the structural elements that forged new economies and, with them, new consumer markets. In marketing the racially inflected performances to particular audiences, various media emphasized racial otherness, using it as a direct selling point and shorthand signifier. And while, as mentioned above, Williams and Walker used racist rhetoric to tout their authenticity to audiences, appropriation and mimicry were every bit as expected by spectators and every bit as profitable. In *Modernist Goods: Primitivism, the Market, and the Gift* (2008), Glenn Willmott argues that "the symptomatic gambit of a modern primitivism" is "to muster resources in order to *speculate* upon its own non-market future, to transvalue the agencies and things of realms it has enveloped in exploitation and commodification, into utopian goods of its own" (5–6). As we saw in the case of Libby Holman's torch songs, these racial dynamics were never unattached to matters of gender and sexuality. Scheper speaks to this phenomenon in relation to, for example, the blues: "In the marketing drive to make blues more 'palatable' . . . for white audiences, white singers often made use of forms of cultural appropriation, in which black female subjectivity and experience 'circulate within the marketplace only when they can be packaged within a real or illusory white woman's body'" (99).

In 1896—the year that *Plessy v. Ferguson* was decided in the Supreme Court, upholding segregation's constitutionality, and the year that William and Walker brought the cakewalk to popular audiences—a significant moment of a very different sort occurred on the modern stage when three African American opera singers joined forces for a performance at Carnegie Hall. Each a famous soprano in her own right, Marie Selika Williams, Flora Batson, and Sissieretta Jones received introduction to the public in one way or another by virtue of both racial otherness and proximity to an authorizing figure. The press called Batson "the colored Jenny Lind," after the Swedish opera singer, while Jones was known to her audiences as "the Black Patti," invoking the Italian opera singer Adelina Patti. Williams, meanwhile, carried the distinction of being the first black artist to perform at the White House (for Rutherford B. Hayes and his wife in 1878)—upon introduction by none other than Frederick Douglass. Paul Robeson would later attempt to shift the perspective that saw black American performers as inheritors of Anglo-European cultural traditions and artistic forms. In relation to tenor and composer Roland Hayes (1887–1977), Robeson suggested the following: "One of great measures of a people is its culture. Above all things, we boast that the only true artistic contributions of America are Negro in origin. We boast of the culture of ancient Africa" (Swindall 42). The incorporation of, comparison to, and distancing from European performance traditions and genres are, of course, part of a complex series of exchanges between performers of color and nations whose colonial pasts made complicated appearances in their modernist contexts.

The innovations happening within black artistic circles signaled variation and multiplicity, implicitly rejecting a singularly "black" mode of sounding or performing even while facilitating Robeson's point about black aesthetic contributions. In *Epistrophes: Jazz and the Literary Imagination* (2017), for example, Brent Hayes Edwards poses the ways in which black writers and musicians in the modernist era crosshatched sound/music and writing/language, experimenting with one by way of the other. In so doing, he suggests that "pseudomorphosis—working one medium in the shape of or in the shadow of another—is the paradigm of innovation in black art" (19). Focusing on the manifestations of these experimental forms in more overtly political spaces, Matthew Hart takes the discussion of modernist performances of race into the realm of ethno-national speech and writing in his *Nations of Nothing But Poetry: Modernism, Transnationalism, and Synthetic Vernacular Writing* (2010).

Thus, where representations of race, gender, and sexuality intersected into a selling point that highlighted difference and a way of literally owning it, some performers made use of the spaces between repetitions and representations to deviate and offer ideas about different and better social roles for people of color. In *Staging Race*, Karen Sotiropoulos points to the sociopolitical idealism of black contributions to popular culture in the early twentieth century:

> In the *business* of fantasy, dreams, and imagination, and coming of age with the rise of Jim Crow, turn-of-the-century black performers envisioned a better place. With a mix of African-descended and American-lived culture, their creative moment was a hybrid one—a bricolage—of European classics, American minstrelsy, *The Wonderful Wizard of Oz*, and the "souls of black folk" (242, emphasis ours).

As our next section will show, some performers—as well as athletes—
used their popularity to contest limited and limiting definitions of race.
In some cases, this took the shape of provocative and unapologetic
counterexamples to white stereotypes and black expectations alike.
In other cases, these celebrities amassed awareness of the structural
discriminations and injustices faced by people of color.

Activism

In *Blues Legacies and Black Feminism* (1998), Angela Davis talks
about the evocative blurring between the personal and political
in blues music: "There is . . . a significant number of women's blues
songs on work, jail, prostitution, natural disasters, and other issues
that, when taken together, constitute a patchwork social history of
black Americans during the decades following emancipation. Most
often such themes are intertwined with themes of love and sexuality"
(91). In a chapter on Bessie Smith and Ma Rainey, Davis traces the
socially conscious work of these blues women, calling Smith's "Poor
Man Blues," for example, a "venerable but forgotten ancestor of the
social protest genre in black popular music" and "Washwoman's Blues"
"a powerfully moving tribute to the countless numbers of African-
American women whose toiling hands released their more prosperous
white sisters from the drudgery of domestic work" (97, 102). Rainey's
"Chain Gang Blues," meanwhile, is described as "a deeply felt protest
aimed at the racism and sexism of the criminal justice system" (104).

Inasmuch as these performance endeavors gave consumers
celebrity figures around which their ideas about race could cohere, the

platforms occupied by musicians, dancers, and athletes became critical sites where political activism could take place. In 1888, journalist and activist Ida B. Wells wrote "The Model Woman," invoking public performance as a way to think through the characteristics and implications of this politically minded Negro woman. Daphne A. Brooks describes the piece in *Bodies in Dissent: Spectacular Performances of Race and Freedom, 1850–1910* (2006): "A longtime 'theatre bug,' [Wells] discovered in print culture a way to cultivate public voice and to launch revised images of New Negro womanhood in ways that paralleled a career in theatre" (281). She imagined the figurative spotlight to be newly shone on the person, which would by extension illuminate the platform. As we have suggested in various ways throughout this book, performances have never been far away from politics. One need only look to the theatrical origins of what would become the name of post-Reconstruction segregation laws in the Deep South. "Jim Crow" was the signature character in Thomas Dartmouth ("Daddy") Rice's popular minstrel show whose success peaked in the 1830s and 1840s.

In the domains of music, dance, and theater, black performers showcased their resistance to the racist caricatures of their contemporaries as well as to the political structures more broadly that created a market for consuming them. This was the case both in song/performance themes and in the political lives of the performers themselves. Josephine Baker, for example, refused to perform for segregated audiences, assisted French Resistance during the Second World War, and would later contribute to the civil rights movement. Paul Robeson, meanwhile, involved himself in causes advocating workers' rights and anti-imperialist efforts, supported the Loyalists in the Spanish Civil War in their struggle against fascism—actions and sympathies for which he became blacklisted during the McCarthy era. Robeson also continued to be a vocal presence in the civil rights movement—a late modernist moment that would see many performers joining its ranks, including the complicated figure of Libby Holman who, as discussed above, fancied herself as performing a kind of respectful racial drag in her appropriations and improvizations of black musical styles and traditions.

One of the best-known examples of modernist performance-as-racial-protest is Billie Holiday's popularizing "Strange Fruit," published as a poem in 1937 and then set to song by Abel Meeropol. An anti-lynching protest, the song responded directly to the widespread ritualistic lynchings (public performances all their own) and became a staple in Holiday's shows. She closed with it (and didn't deliver encores) when performing in New York's first integrated nightclub, Café Society, which would go completely dark for the duration of the song, save for a spotlight on Holiday's face. The power of the song became evident not only in the aesthetic machinations that went into staging it but also in its effects off stage. Harry Anslinger, the first commissioner of what was then the relatively still-new Federal Bureau of Narcotics (est. 1930), demanded that Holiday discontinue the song in her performances. When she ignored his order, the Bureau focused attention on her, ultimately entrapping her in a drug sting and imprisoning her. After she was released, the structural racism present in the federal government took shape in an artistic limitation: her cabaret performer's license was not renewed, and nightclubs became off limits.[6]

Expanding the discussion of racial protest and performance, we also want to look at an arena not often associated with traditional aesthetic/creative forms but which nonetheless played a pivotal role in modernist contexts: the sporting arena. Inasmuch as "the campaign for racial equality in sports often inspired and foreshadowed the campaign for racial equality in society," sports icons like Jesse Owens used their fame to make political contributions as well (Lamb 2016, 6). Winning four gold medals at the 1936 Berlin Olympic Games, track phenom Jesse Owens challenged racial myths of white superiority and, by extension, national exceptionalism. Mark Dyreson suggests in his "Prolegomena to Jesse Owens: American Ideas about Race and Olympic Races from the 1890s to the 1920s" that "Owens and his fellow African-American Olympians thus simultaneously symbolized both the process of nation-making and the process of marking racial differences" (225). Looking at the various treatments of Owens in the press, meanwhile, Pamela C. Laucella sets out to think about how "sports journalists use[d] language to create, attribute, or sustain the persona of Jesse Owens" (53).

In interesting contradistinction to Owens's humble demeanor, Jack Johnson gave fodder to reporters, politicians, and other public figures that would allow the discussion about race and performance to be framed in radically different ways. His complicated (and at times, outright contrary) relationship to ideas about racial uplift drew criticism from all corners, despite simultaneously establishing him as a paragon of strength. The first African American world heavyweight boxing champion, Johnson, held the title from 1908 to 1915. Phillip J. Hutchison opens his essay "Framing White Hopes: The Press, Social Drama, and the Era of Jack Johnson, 1908–1915" with a particularly telling quote describing Johnson's 1910 fight with "Great White Hope" James J. Jeffries: "No other single event dug so deep into world consciousness until the Lindbergh flight seventeen years later. . . . This was the first great modern happening; it was the first great media morality play" (19).[7] Like Billie Holiday, Johnson was targeted by the government at the height of his success, and he was ultimately convicted in 1913 of violating the Mann Act, which forbade "transporting women across state lines for immoral purposes." Johnson had already sparked controversy for his relationships with white women and his fondness for prostitutes. He also, as mentioned earlier, opened a nightclub in Harlem in 1920 that would a few years later become the famous Cotton Club. His successes and excesses predictably inflamed racist indignation from white people, which played into the easy drama that unfolded as Jeffries (with compulsion from promoters and the press who knew what a story it would make, how many tickets and papers would sell) came out of retirement to challenge Johnson's title. As Hutchison notes, "A black man rightly laid claim to a cherished title that over decades had been crafted—largely in the press—as the epitome of masculinity and civilization" (26).

In this period in which civilization rhetoric was met with racial uplift and respectability politics, however, Johnson attracted criticism not only from white racists but also from African Americans seeking to make social and economic progress. Perhaps most significant was the sharp critique issued by a disappointed Booker T. Washington, who opined what a shame it was "that a man with money should use it in a way to injure his own people in the eyes of those who are seeking to uplift his race and improve its conditions. . . . I wish to say emphatically that Jack Johnson's actions did not meet my personal approval and I am sure they do not meet with the approval of the colored race" (Morgan 538).[8] Thus Johnson's "activism" did not come in the form of championing a community of brethren but in his openly defying racialized expectations, no matter their source. Whatever one might say about his contraventions of social norms, however, performances inside and outside the ring—and how they came to be narrativized in the press—established a Jack Johnson created by the interests of those around him. With an emphasis on the media structures and their story arcs at the time, Hutchison puts it as follows: "Despite the complexity of the Johnson situation, the white press was able to construct the boxer's social presence in terms of an overarching narrative framework that structured—and in effect contained—news reportage for nearly seven years" (39). It hardly works, then, to seek out some "man behind the myth." The man *was* the myth, and the myth was the man.

Thinking outward

The inextricable relationship between aesthetics/performance, politics, and identity is not unique to the modern era, of course. Generations earlier, spirituals sung on plantations served as subversive organizing tactics. Generations later, hip-hop would usher in a musical performance genre as lucrative as it is subversive. Worth keeping in mind as well, of course, is the fact that white American and Anglo-European aesthetic traditions and innovations have never been apolitical or content neutral either. As we have tried to demonstrate, colonial investments and white anxieties are often thinly veiled in canonical modernist works. The dominance of those texts, however, also afforded them a different kind of critical discussion—one that would present them as context-free inheritors of a monolithic tradition whose exclusions and presumptions were seen as incidental if not altogether unimportant (if they came into the discussion in the first place). In this manner, "race" in modernist contexts was long thought to apply only to people of color who contributed to and innovated within those spaces. New modernist interventions have inaugurated more complicated scholarly renderings of the political and ideological investments at work in canon formation, as well as those necessary for canon disruption. These themes—of tradition, hegemony, politics, aesthetics, identity, and critique—are still prevalent today, of course. Our Coda will offer a brief consideration of how identifications of race and "progress" (once at the root of discourse on modernism, now at the root of discourse on technology and globalization) continue to shape one another.

Notes

1 See *Black Cultural Traffic: Crossroads in Global Performance and Popular Culture*, Harry J. Elam, Jr., and Kennell Jackson, eds. (Ann Arbor: U of Michigan P, 2005), 148.

2 Printed in 1911 by Kenny Publishing Company in New York, this text is now available through the University of Connecticut Libraries' digital archives: https://archive.org/details/monarchsofminstr00rice

3 See Arjun Appadurai's *Modernity at Large: Cultural Dimensions of Globalization* (Minneapolis: U of Minnesota P, 1996).

4 See Rashida K. Braggs, *Jazz Diasporas: Race Music and Migration in Post-World War II Paris* (Oakland: U of California P, 2016).

5 See the New York art critic Clement Greenberg's classic 1939 essay "Avant-Garde and Kitsch," which was published in *Partisan Review*.

6 With her career halted, Holiday slipped back into drug use and was ultimately hospitalized. Even then, Anslinger continued his antagonism.

He sent his men to the hospital, where they handcuff her to the bed and prevented the doctors' methadone treatments. She died within days. For a discussion of the relationship between race politics and drug legislation and how it played out in Billie Holiday's short life, see Johann Hari's *Chasing the Scream: The First and Last Days of the War on Drugs* (London: Bloomsbury, 2015).

7 See Lerone Bennett's April 1994 *Ebony* article "Jack Johnson and the Great White Hope," 86–98.

8 Denise C. Morgan, "Jack Johnson: Reluctant Hero of the Black Community." *Akron Law Review*. 32.3 (1999): 529–56.

Coda—Who's the Matter?

We end this book where we began: with a recent book telling a story about the slave trade that attends to, among other things, the roles played by Africans in the buying and selling of other Africans. While Hurston focuses in *Barracoon* on the final punctuating voice of one person's story, offering her own rendering of the last first-person account of the Middle Passage, Yaa Gyasi's *Homegoing* (2016) tells its tale through two family lines for eight generations. Heralded as an inspiring first novel of a new literary voice, the book received an important endorsement from Ta-Nehisi Coates. In his blurb, Coates, like Walker in her foreword to *Barracoon*, suggests that one important achievement of the book is its boldly facing African participation in the slave trade, its looking historical culpability in the eye: "Gyasi is deeply concerned with the sin of selling humans on Africans, not Europeans. But she does not scold. She does not excuse. And she does not romanticize. The black Americans she follows are not overly virtuous victims. Sin comes in all forms, from selling people to abandoning children."

In a 2016 interview with Isaac Chotiner for *Slate*, Gyasi draws an important parallel between *Homegoing* and contemporary

American race politics. The novel follows the respective generational lines of an Asante woman's two daughters, one of whom marries a British slave trader who serves as governor for one of the commercial forts on the Gold Coast, and the other is sold into slavery from that same fort. It is a sweeping story, traversing centuries and continents. However, as she tells Chotiner, Gyasi's starting point was much more contemporaneous and local: "When I started the book, I was thinking about this broad question of what it means to be black in America. . . . That's why I wanted to get to these immigrant characters." Despite belonging to different genres and very different contexts, *Barracoon* and *Homegoing* are telling examples of two authors' unsentimental refusals to distinguish aesthetics and politics, present and past, individual and community, violence and volition, nation and migration, race and identity.

These coextensive dynamics—critical to modernist conceptions and performances of "race"—continue to frame contemporary discussions and analyses of subjectivity. It should come as no surprise, then, that *Barracoon* has been met with both broadscale and enthusiastic praise in 2018, despite not being able to find an audience when Hurston wrote it. However, despite the kinds of analytical inroads made in the last thirty-or-so years, the impulse to classify with clear and fixed boundaries remains a strong one where these concepts play out in contemporary political and popular culture. Bringing our discussion of modernist moments into the present allows us to think about the contingency of race, about how racial formations and classifications continue simultaneously to constitute and challenge each other, and about the ways our identifications tell us more about our own investments and expectations than they do about what we attempt to name.

I

In the summer of 2015, the head of the National Association for the Advancement of Colored People (NAACP) Spokane chapter and noted civil rights worker Rachel Dolezal—an African American woman, as far as all her friends and colleagues knew—became the subject of immense controversy when her birth mother Ruthanne confirmed that her daughter had been born Caucasian. Dolezal's own claims about her connection to black culture only further clouded the truth—she falsely identified a black man named Albert Wilkerson as her biological father, for example. After the story broke, however, the matter received quick consensus in American public opinion: Rachel Dolezal was a white woman attempting to "pass" as African American. After quick and broad ridicule (as well as a book deal for her and a documentary), the story on Dolezal seemed to fade into the ethers, especially as a presidential campaign season was in full swing—significantly, one in which one candidate was endorsed by former KKK grand wizard David Duke and the other had famously used the term "super-predators" to talk about black youth. However, Dolezal's unique story invokes the complicated ways in which race, identity, and modernism have been construed after the post-structuralist turn. Complicating the matter further, Dolezal had worked much of her life to articulate the oppressions African Americans face and to work to fight against them. She had been a tireless advocate for Black Lives Matter, and she devoted her professional life as an advocate for racial equality.

The Dolezal controversy presents difficult but useful questions for scholars of modernism and race in is postmodern moment. How can scholars adhere to social constructionism and avoid invoking a stable or knowable "history" or "identity" in relation to the high-stakes contexts of race and identification? In what ways have notions of race as a biological marker continued to proliferate in contemporary media and academic outlets, and how do these notions serve competing interests? What are we to make of the phenomenon of Rachel Dolezal's calling the constructionists' bluff in the context of police brutality against African Americans? What kinds of value—heuristic or otherwise—do signifiers like "blackness" and "modernity" continue to hold, and for whom? In what ways do these contemporary moments rely upon some of the same questions and debates emphasized in the modernist era?

This story of racial self-identification and its fallout provides a good (albeit troubling) example of how relatively static definitions of race have remained since modernist artists first began grappling with them more than a century ago. In his book *Trans: Gender and Race in an Age of Unsettled Identities* (2016), Rogers Brubaker examines Dolezal's outing as "white" and her claims of being "transracial" alongside Caitlyn Jenner's widely celebrated transition that same year—announced with the "Call me Caitlyn" cover of *Vanity Fair*. In comparing the two cases, Brubaker notes that, while "subjective gender identity" represents "a socially legitimate basis for . . . chang[ing] the way one is identified by others" as a valid position, "the authority of ancestry over racial classification in North America" makes it impossible to claim an alternate race without it being read as "getting others to *misperceive* that race" (7).

Brubaker offers "trans" as a suggestive rhetorical tool that can assist attempts to think through identifications of race and gender and the occasions for deploying essentialist, voluntarist, or constructionist logics in those identifications. He offers three domains—the trans of migration, the trans of between, and the trans of beyond—to demonstrate the fluidity of racial identification in the twenty-first century:

> Each form . . . can help us think about race and ethnicity in fruitful ways. Racial passing (including "reverse passing" like Dolezal's) exemplifies the trans of migration, the multiracial movement illustrates the trans of between, and indifference or opposition to racial or ethnic categorization is an instance of the trans of beyond. (11)

The rhetoric and practice of passing are no simpler or less ideologically fraught now than they were during the Harlem Renaissance. Ultimately they confront us with the politics of classification—the effects of which shape the realities of social life. Taking serious stock of the ways in which rhetoric fashions reality, we can complicate notions of "matter" as some kind of biologically determined entity and focus instead on how "matter" is deemed and determined. In other words, who's the matter?

The discursive possibilities of "trans" suggest studies of race and new modernism are not only literary and historical but also epistemological efforts. The politically dueling claims in America that "Black Lives Matter" and "*All* lives matter" are a case in point. There are obvious assumptions and ideological positions that have to be up and running in order for the latter slogan to be offered as a counter to the first, as well as for the two to play competing roles politically. The fact that a contingent of Americans felt the need to present a response to the claim that "black lives matter" (itself prompted by George Zimmerman's 2013 acquittal after killing black teenager Trayvon Martin) in the first place, of course, gives rise to the question of what kind of anxiety must be operative to motivate that response. That naming black life as a matter of concern and value prompted such anxiety is suggestive of the discomfort caused within dominant structures and sectors when racial otherness is identified as a space of autonomous political action and voice. That such discomfort is caused is suggestive of the contingency and tenuousness of the category "whiteness," such that people are quick to police its boundaries and reify its value as a significant marker of identity.

The critical work coming from the best strands of new modernist inquiry asks us to think about who gets excluded in universalizing appeals to "all lives." Taking serious stock of the politics of classification asks us to identify the boundary maintenance happening in the name of liberal humanism. The same kinds of boundary maintenance were also at work, of course, when black American football star Colin Kaepernick decided to kneel during the national anthem before games to protest structural racism in the United States. Critical responses to his actions laid claim to a nebulous "patriotism" that stood in for very specific social and ideological allegiances. The notion of a sweeping humankind to which we all belong, of course, did important work for Anglo-European modernists who made invocations to a grand "tradition" or an ideal "aesthetics," and it continues to do important work for those who would turn to a widespread colorblindness in order to mute articulations of racial and contextual (not to mention historical) specificity.

The obsession many of those same modernists had with exploring themes in their creative work through what they deemed "exotic" or "primitive" remains resonant today, too, with musicians like Miley Cyrus and Justin Timberlake sparking accusations of exploiting the black musical and cultural forms that they have used in fashioning their own brands. Again, the boundaries drawn by acts of classification were and remain at work: Where does appreciation stop and appropriation begin?

On a more structural level, identifications of race and the consequences thereof are what have been at work at the end of the Civil War, when personhood was (at least nominally) extended to those who had been classified as "property." These identifications and their consequences have been at work in the modernist moment of Jim Crow laws that used "white" and "colored" as direct signifiers of access and ostracism. They have been at work in a "war on drugs" implicitly signaling and overtly resulting in a war on poor communities of color. They have been at work in the Bush speechwriter David Frum's designation of an "axis of evil" in the Middle East and the foreign policies that followed. They remain at work in the statistical disparity with which Ava DuVernay opens her powerful documentary *13th*: namely, the United States is home to 5 percent of the world's population and 25 percent of the world's prisoners. Dismantling the fiction that would present a story of that statistic as an unfortunate coincidence or, more insidiously, as evidence of a propensity for criminality in communities of color, DuVernay offers a close reading of the language in the

Thirteenth Amendment that outlawed slavery and servitude "except as punishment for a crime." In so doing, she presents an incisive look at the racialized codifications of violence, addiction, and predation that have resulted in a dramatically disproportionate number of imprisoned people of color in a system that profits from their incarceration.

Lest the Dolezal controversy, Colin Kaepernick protest, popular music, and the prison industrial complex appear as isolated cultural moments, they are all extensions of naming practices that identify an "us" and a "them," an "insider" and an "outsider," and the subsequent processes of maintaining or attempting to traverse the boundaries around those subject positions. Those same identifications were at the heart of aesthetic and political projects in the first half of the twentieth century. It perhaps should come as no surprise, then, that modernist figures have reemerged in contemporary discourses on race, art, and politics. The year 2016 saw the release of *I Am Not Your Negro*, a documentary based on some of the late writings of James Baldwin. Significantly, Baldwin work continues to stand as an arbiter of the power of names and what they reveal. He famously discussed, for example, the n-word as an invention that has nothing to do with the person to which it is assigned and everything to do with the psychology, experiences, and expectations of the person deploying the term.[1] Meanwhile, as already discussed, Zora Neale Hurston's work has been back in the public spotlight with the release of *Barracoon*. The phenomenon of a Harlem Renaissance author, writing about a former African slave, being published in twenty-first-century America, in fact, makes all too much sense.

II

We are back here.

Because we have organized many of our chapters around geospatial sites during specific historical moments, we would like to close this book with a consideration of the site where we found ourselves completing it: two next-door offices in which we worked at the National Humanities Center in Durham, North Carolina, in the summer of 2018. For the month of June, we started each day with a short drive from the hotel to our offices. Our conversations—in the car, over lunch, at dinner—would often turn to the book, of course: what we were writing or planning to write, how we would approach structure or frame a particular discussion. But much of our time together—on our ways to and from the offices, as we ate meals—was spent grappling with what we were seeing and hearing on the news every morning: the explosion of images of children forcibly separated from their parents at the US-Mexico border.

One level of response to those images and sounds—viscerally felt but of little analytical value—involved disappointed hand wringing and sympathetic humanism that appeals to the value of all people everywhere. But another level of response and critique—one that presses the implications of social theory—offered a challenge to think structurally about the kinds of categories that made such images and sounds possible. Certain definitions had to be up and running—namely, those of "immigrant," "illegal," "border," "citizen," "detention," and "asylum," just to name a few. The discourses in which such definitions operate are not simply moments of semantic claptrap overlooking the *real* or *authentic* meanings of those terms. Indeed, those categories have never been removed from ideological investments. It is not coincidental or innocuous, for example, that one of the responses to this policy from white progressives suggested that European ancestors were themselves immigrants. The choice of the term "immigrants" rather than, say, "colonialists" does important work for the attempt at a universalizing embrace of humankind. To put it more bluntly, children of color have long been separated from their families by powerful governments. The politics of classification have always been at work—in colonial projects, in segregation laws, and in for-profit prison systems.

For these and other reasons, we are committed to pursuing the questions to which social theory gives rise, some of which have guided our discussion throughout this book. They are questions about how people go about naming and organizing their social worlds—offering and operationalizing definitions of borders, migration, lines, segregation, folk, empire, whiteness, and otherness, and manufacturing them in the process. How these categories come to be created and contested, then, is a matter of modernist aesthetics and politics, as well as of contemporary social discourse. In the same way that modernist conventions of aesthetic and tradition pointed toward a thinly veiled notion of Anglo-European global dominance, current definitions of "citizen" and "immigrant" are more to do with power dynamics foundational to the American nation-state than they are to do with the ontological status of either of those designations.

Because a naming process says more about the namer than the thing being named, any story about "race and new modernism" must reckon with the Anglocentric rubrics that guided early twentieth-century understandings of identity and otherness. These rubrics not only shaped new avenues for artistic innovation but also facilitated nationalist projects, racial stereotypes, and economic disenfranchisements. They stoked fear and anxiety during a time when black men were being lynched in the southern United States, and they articulated anti-Semitism en route to the Holocaust. These rubrics were not modernism's anomalous failures—they were its characterizing features. Figures who participated in such projects— like Ezra Pound—still loom large in the modernist canon. It is simultaneously crucial to point out, however, that the slippages in the repetitions of modernist racial performance also allowed for revisions, such as Billie Holiday's popularizing a protest song about lynching at the same time modernist rhetorics of civilization were deployed in the hanging rituals.

We would be remiss if we ended this book without asking, then—in the 1920s American South, or the 1930s in Harlem, or 1903 in Paris, or 1899 in Puerto Rico, or, indeed, 2018 in North Carolina, or whatever year and spot you are in as you read this volume—what slippages and fault lines in the performances of race and modernism have seen revisions such that those engaged in their discourses might see the various ways in which the tropes constitute and contest one another? Frequently, we come to those sites and moments wanting to identify each as a unique or special case. And while contextual and historical specificity is certainly key, we must beware of the temptation to avoid structural critique that would ask challenging but important questions about the ideological work of rhetoric—the work it has done in the past and the work it continues to do.

In this manner, when it comes to the consequences of how we go about processes of naming, marketing, performing, and consuming, there is not so much a linear trajectory as there is an elliptical orbit. Indeed, W. E. B. Du Bois's claim to a European audience that the century was facing a problem of "the color line" was not irreducibly relevant to 1900. Steve Bannon's claim to the National Front in France—that the labels "racists," "xenophobes," and "nativists" are to be worn "as a badge of honor"—demonstrates as much. The color line has always reflected a classification line, after all: one that demarcates, excludes or includes, and draws perimeters in the service of specific interests. Consequently, Zora Neale Hurston, as both an author and a concept, is as much a contemporary phenomenon as a modernist one. The rhetoric of *newness* in both periods, of course, is really about what is old. Ezra Pound's clarion call to "make it *new*" was about reinvigorating and reinventing what he deemed important about the past, championing a very particular vision of civilization by way of aesthetic exactitude (and, by extension, exclusivity). Meanwhile, *new* modernist studies has offered innovation by way of old themes. The field has been a productive framework in which scholars employ, among other things, the critical tools that modernist writers and artists of color had long been presenting in their own work. Specifically, the new modernist approach to discourse on aesthetics— that it is never about art alone but instead about the entanglements of power and privilege surrounding the artist—is not a revelation. It is a reality readily and emphatically available in so many of works from the modernist period that specifically attend to race. A primary importance of new modernist studies lies in its ability to showcase in analytically sophisticated ways what *Barracoon* demonstrates by virtue of its 2018 publication: namely, everything old may be new again, but the new has always been older than it seems.

How far have we come?

How far will we go?

We are back here.

KMS

JAC

DURHAM, NC 2018

Note

1   See him talk about that idea here: https://www.youtube.com/watch?v=L0L 5fciA6AU

WORKS CITED

Adams, Jessica, Michael P. Bibler, and Cécile Accilien, eds. *Just Below South: Intercultural Performance in the Caribbean and the U.S. South.* The U of Virginia P, 2007.

Appadurai, Arjun. *Modernity at Large: Cultural Dimensions of Globalization.* U of Minnesota P, 1996.

Ayers, David. "Wyndham Lewis and the Modernists: Internationalism and Race," in *Modernism and Race*, Lenn Platt, ed. Cambridge UP, 2011: 156–172.

Azéradt, Hugues. "Édouard Glissant and the Text of Faulkner's Modernism." *American Creoles: The Francophone Caribbean and the American South.* Edited by Martin Munro and Celia Britton. Liverpool UP, 2012. 197–215.

_____. *Blues, Ideology, and Afro-American Literature: A Vernacular Theory.* U of Chicago P, 1984.

_____. *Modernism and the Harlem Renaissance.* U of Chicago P, 1987.

Baker, Houston A., Jr. *Turning South Again: Re-Thinking Modernism/Re-Reading Booker T.* Duke UP, 2001.

Baker, Houston A., Jr. and Dana D. Nelson "Violence, the Body and 'The South.'" *American Literature.* 73.2 (June 2001). 231–244.

Baker, Houston A., Jr. and K. Merinda Simmons, eds. *The Trouble with Post-Blackness.* Columbia UP, 2015.

Baraka, Amiri. *Blues People: Negro Music in White America.* 1963. Harper Perennial, 1999.

Bayart, Jean-Francᛉois. *The Illusion of Cultural Identity.* U of Chicago P, 2005.

Beasley, Rebecca. "Modernism's Translations." *The Oxford Handbook of Global Modernisms.* Mark Wollaeger and Matt Eatough, eds. Oxford UP, 2012. 551–570.

Bennett, Lerone. "Jack Johnson and the Great White Hope." *Ebony* (April 1994): 86–98.

Bone, Martyn. "The (Extended) South of Black Folk: Intraregional and Transnational Migrant Labor in *Jonah's Gourd Vine* and *Their Eyes Were Watching God.*" *American Literature.* 79.4 (2007): 753–779.

_____. *Where the New World Is: Literature about The U.S. South at Global Scales.* U of Georgia P, 2018.

Booth, Howard J., and Nigel Rigby. *Modernism and Empire: Writing and British Coloniality, 1890-1940.* Manchester UP, 2000.

Braggs, Rashida K. *Jazz Diasporas: Race, Music, and Migration in Post-World War II Paris.* U of California P, 2016.

Brawley, Benjamin G. *The Negro in Literature and Art in the United States* (1918). Reprinted CreateSpace Independent Publishing Platform, 2015.

Brooks, Cleanth. *An Approach to Literature.* Pearson College Div., 1936, 1976.

Brooks, Cleanth and Robert Penn Warren, eds. *Understanding Poetry.* Holt Rinehart and Winston, 1938, 1976.

Brooks, Daphne A. *Bodies in Dissent: Spectacular Performances of Race and Freedom, 1850-1910.* Durham: Duke UP, 2006.

Brouillette, Sarah. *Postcolonial Writers and the Global Literary Marketplace.* Palgrave Macmillan, 2007.

Brubaker, Rogers. *Trans: Gender and Race in an Age of Unsettled Identities.* Princeton UP, 2016.

Bush, Christopher. *Ideographic Modernism: China, Writing, Media.* Oxford UP, 2010.

Butler, Judith. "Imitation and Gender Insubordination." *The Lesbian and Gay Studies Reader.* Henry Abelove, Michèle Aina Barale, and David M. Halperin, eds. Routledge, 1999: 307–320.

———. *Bodies that Matter: On the Discursive Limits of Sex.* New York: Routledge, 1993.

———. *Gender Trouble: Feminism and the Subversion of Identity.* New York: Routledge, 1990.

Carr, Helen. "Imagism and Empire" in *Modernism and Empire: Writing and British Coloniality 1890-1940*, Nigel Rigby and Howard J. Booth, eds. Manchester UP, 2000: 64–92.

Childs, Donald J. *Modernism and Eugenics: Woolf, Eliot, Yeats, and the Culture of Degeneration.* Cambridge UP, 2001.

Chrisman, Laura. *Postcolonial Contraventions: Cultural Readings of Race, Imperialism and Transnationalism.* Manchester UP, 2003.

Chu, Patricia E. *Race, Nationalism and the State in British and American Modernism.* Cambridge UP, 2006.

Clukey, Amy, and Jeremy Wells. "Introduction: Plantation Modernity." *Global South.* Edited by Amy Clukey and Jeremy Wells. 10.2 (2016): 1–10.

Cohen, Robin, and Paola Toninato, eds. *The Creolization Reader: Studies in Mixed Identities and Cultures.* Routledge, 2010.

Cohn, Deborah. *History and Memory in Two Souths: Recent Southern and Spanish American Fiction.* Vanderbilt UP, 1999.

Cohn, Deborah and Jon Smith, editors. *Look Away!: The U.S. South in New World Studies.* Duke UP, 2004.

Conrad, Joseph. *Heart of Darkness.* Serial in *Blackwood's Magazine.* Feb.–Apr., 1899.

_____. *The Nigger of the "Narcissus."* Heinemann, 1897.

Courtman, Sandra. "From Mary Prince to Joan Riley: Women Writers and the 'Casual Cruelty' of a West Indian Childhood." *Postcolonial Traumas: Memory, Narrative, Resistance,* Abigail Ward, ed. Palgrave Macmillan, 2015. 30–47.

Curtin, Philip D. *The Rise and Fall of the Plantation Complex.* Cambridge UP, 1990.

Dalleo, Raphael. *Caribbean Literature and the Public Sphere: From the Plantation to the Postcolonial.* U of Virginia P, 2011.

Davis, Angela. *Blues Legacies and Black Feminism.* Vintage Books, 1998.

Davis, David A. *World War I and Southern Modernism.* UP of Mississippi, 2017.

Davis, Gerald L. *I Got the Word in Me and I Can Sing It, You Know: A Study of the Performed African-American Sermon.* U of Pennsylvania P, 1987.

Dayan, Colin. *The Law Is a White Dog: How Legal Rituals Make and Unmake Persons.* Princeton UP, 2013.

Douglas, Ann. *Terrible Honesty: Mongrel Manhattan in the 1920s.* Farrar, Straus and Giroux, 1995.

Doyle, Arthur Conan. *The Hound of the Baskervilles.* George Newnes, 1902.

Du Bois, W.E.B. *The Souls of Black Folk.* 1903. Oxford UP, 2014.

Duck, Leigh Anne. *The Nation's Region: Southern Modernism, Segregation, and U.S. Nationalism.* U of Georgia P, 2006.

Duck, Leigh Anne. "Rebirth of a Nation: Hurston in Haiti." *The Journal of American Folklore.* 117.464 (2004):127–146.

Dunbar, Eve. *Black Regions of the Imagination: African American Writers Between the Nation and the World.* Temple UP, 2013.

Dyreson, Mark. "Prolegomena to Jesse Owens: American Ideas About Race and Olympic Races from the 1890s to the 1920s." *The International Journal of the History of Sport.* 25.2 (2008): 224–246.

Edwards, Brent Hayes. *Epistrophes: Jazz and the Literary Imagination.* Cambridge, Harvard UP: 2017.

Edwards, Brent Hayes. *The Practice of Diaspora: Literature, Translation, and the Rise of Black Internationalism.* Harvard UP, 2003.

Einstein, Carl. "On Primitive Art." *October.* 105 (Summer 2003): 124.

Elam, Harry J, et al. *Black Cultural Traffic: Crossroads in Global Performance and Popular Culture.* U of Michigan P, 2005.

Eliot, T.S. "Tradition and the Individual Talent" in *Selected Essays, 1917–1932.* Harcourt: 1932.

Ellison, Ralph. "Recent Negro Fiction." *New Masses.* 40.6 (Aug. 5, 1940): 22–26.

Emery, Mary Lou. *Modernism, the Visual, and Caribbean Literature.* Cambridge UP, 2007.

Etherington, Ben. *Literary Primitivism.* Stanford UP, 2017.

Fanon, Frantz. *Black Skin, White Masks*. Pluto Press, 1954. Translated by Charles Lam Markmann, Grove Press, 1967.

Faulkner, William. *Absalom, Absalom!* Vintage, 1990.

———. *Light in August*. Vintage, 1990.

———. *Requiem for a Nun*. Vintage, 2012.

———. *The Sound and The Fury*. Vintage, 1990.

Ferguson, Dutton. "Twenty-Five Years and Beyond." *Opportunity: Journal of Negro Life*. 25.5 (Fall 1947): 188.

Flannery, Eóin. *Ireland and Postcolonial Studies: Theory, Discourse, Utopia*. Palgrave Macmillan, 2009.

Foley, Barbara. *Jean Toomer: Race, Repression, and Revolution*. U of Illinois P, 2014.

Forbes, Camille F. *Introducing Bert Williams: Burnt Cork, Broadway, and the Story of America's First Black Star*. Basic Civitas, 2008.

Gates, Henry Louis, Jr. *Figures in Black: Words, Signs, and the Racial Self*. Oxford UP, 1989.

———. *The Signifying Monkey: A Theory of African-American Literary Criticism*. Oxford UP, 1988.

Gates, Henry Louis, Jr. "The Trope of a New Negro and the Reconstruction of the Image of the Black." *Representations* No. 24, Special Issue: America Reconstructed, 1840-1940 (Autumn, 1988): 129–155.

Gikandi, Simon. "Picasso, Africa, and the Schemeta of Difference" in *Beautiful/Ugly: African and Diaspora Aesthetics*, Sarah Nuttall, ed. Duke UP, 2006: 30–59.

Gilroy, Paul. *The Black Atlantic: Modernity and Double Consciousness*. Harvard UP, 1993.

Glissant, Édouard. *Faulkner, Mississippi*. Chicago UP, 1996.

Golston, Michael. *Rhythm and Race in Modernist Poetry and Science: Pound, Yeats, Williams, and Modernist Sciences of Rhythm*. Columbia UP, 2007.

Gottschild, Brenda Dixon. *Digging the Africanist Presence in American Performance*. Greenwood Press, 1996.

Greenberg, Clement. "Avant-Garde and Kitsch." *Partisan Review*. 6 (Fall 1939): 34–49.

Guridy, Frank Andre. *Forging Diaspora. Afro-Cubans and African Americans in a World of Empire and Jim Crow*. U of North Carolina P, 2010.

Gyasi, Yaa. *Homegoing*. Alfred A. Knopf, 2016.

Hall, Catherine. *White, Male, and Middle-Class: Explorations in Feminism and History*. Routledge, 1992.

Handley, George B. *Postslavery Literatures in the Americas: Family Portraits in Black and White*. UP of Virginia, 2000.

Hari, Johann. *Chasing the Scream: The First and Last Days of the War on Drugs*. London: Bloomsbury, 2015.

Harris, Trudier. *The Scary Mason-Dixon Line: African American Writers and the South*. Louisiana State UP, 2009.

____. *Summer Snow: Reflections from a Black Daughter of the South*. Beacon Press, 2003.

Hart, Matthew. *Nations of Nothing But Poetry: Modernism, Transnationalism, and Synthetic Vernacular Writing*. Oxford UP, 2010.

Hayot, Eric. "Chinese Modernism, Mimetic Desire, and European Time." *The Oxford Handbook of Global Modernisms*. Mark A. Wollaeger and Matt Eatough, eds. Oxford UP, 2012. 149–172.

Hemingway, Ernest. *A Moveable Feast: The Restored Edition*. New York: Scribner, 1964 (2009).

____. *The Sun Also Rises*. Scribner's, 1926.

Hobson, Fred. *The Southern Writer in the Postmodern World*. U of Georgia P, 1991.

Holloway, Joseph E., ed. *Africanisms in American Culture*. Indiana UP, 1990.

Huggan, Graham. *The Postcolonial Exotic: Marketing the Margins*. Routledge, 2001.

Huggins, Nathan Irvin. *Harlem Renaissance*. Oxford UP, 1971.

Hughes, Langston. *The Big Sea: An Autobiography*. 1940. Hill and Wang, 1993.

____. *The Weary Blues*. Alfred A. Knopf, 1926.

Hurston, Zora Neale. *Barracoon: The Story of the Last "Black Cargo."* HarperCollins, 2018.

____. "How It Feels to be a Colored Me" in *The Norton Anthology of African American Literature* Nellie Y. McKay and Henry Louis Gates, eds. Norton & Co, 2003.

____. *Mules and Men*. J. B. Lippincott Co., 1935.

____. *Tell My Horse: Voodoo and Life in Haiti and Jamaica*. HarperCollins, 1938.

Hurston, Zora Neale. *Their Eyes Were Watching God*. J. P. Lippincott, 1937.

Hutchinson, Ben. *Modernism and Style*. Palgrave Macmillan, 2011.

Hutchinson, George. *The Harlem Renaissance in Black and White*. Belknap Press, 1995.

Hutchison, Phillip J. "Framing White Hopes: The Press, Social Drama, and the Era of Jack Johnson, 1908-1915." *From Jack Johnson to LeBron James: Sports, Media, and the Color Line*, edited by Chris Lamb. Lincoln: U of Nebraska P, 2016. 19–51.

Jackson, Gale. "The Way We Do: A Preliminary Investigation of the African Roots of African American Performance." *Black American Literature Forum*. 25.1 (Spring 1991): 11–22.

Jackson, Jeffrey. *Making Jazz French: Music and Modern Life in Interwar Paris.* Duke UP, 2003.

Jaffe, Aaron. "Who's Afraid of the Inhuman Woolf?". *Modernism/Modernity.* 23.3 (2016): 491–513.

James, Henry. *Daisy Miller.* Harper & Brothers, 1879.

Jones, E. K. "Cooperation and Opportunity." *Opportunity: Journal of Negro Life.* 25.5 (Fall 1947): 185.

Jones, E. K., ed. *Opportunity.* 2.21 (Sept. 1924): 259.

Kazin, Alfred. *On Native Grounds: An Interpretation of Modern American Prose Literature.* Reynal & Hitchcock, 1942.

King, Richard H. *A Southern Renaissance: The Cultural Awakening of the American South, 1930-1955.* Oxford UP, 1980.

Konzett, Delia Caporoso. *Ethnic Modernisms: Anzia Yezierska, Zora Neale Hurston, Jean Rhys, and the Aesthetic of Dislocation.* Palgrave Macmillan, 2002.

Lamb, Chris. "Introduction." *From Jack Johnson to LeBron James: Sports, Media, and the Color Line,* edited by Chris Lamb. U of Nebraska P, 2016. 1–18.

Lassner, Phyllis: "Race, Gender and the Holocaust: Traumatic Modernity, Traumatic Modernism" in *Modernism and Race,* Lenn Platt, ed. Cambridge UP, 2011: 192–211.

Latham, Sean, and Gayle Rogers. *Modernism: Evolution of An Idea.* Bloomsbury Academic, 2015.

Laucella, Pamela C. "Jesse Owens, a Black Pearl amidst an ocean of Fury: A Case Study of Press Coverage of the 1936 Berlin Olympic Games." *From Jack Johnson to LeBron James: Sports, Media, and the Color Line,* edited by Chris Lamb. Lincoln: U of Nebraska P, 2016. 52–85.

Leiter, Andrew B. *In the Shadow of the Black Beast: African American Masculinity in the Harlem and Southern Renaissances.* Louisiana State UP, 2010.

Leiter, Andrew B.. "Miscegenation and Progression: The First Americans of Jean Toomer and William Faulkner," in *Faulkner and the Black Literatures of the Americas.* Jay Watson and James G. Thomas, eds. Oxford: U of Mississippi P, 2016. 74–88.

Lewis, David Levering. *When Harlem Was in Vogue.* Knopf, 1981.

Lewis, Pericles. *Modernism, Nationalism, and the Novel.* Cambridge UP, 2000.

Locke, Alain. "The New Negro." *The New Negro: Readings on Race, Representation, and African American Culture, 1892-1938.* Henry Louis Gates, Jr and Gene Andrew Jarrett, eds. Princeton UP, 2007. 112–118.

Loichot, Valérie. "Creolizing Barack Obama" in *American Creoles: The Francophone Caribbean and the American South,* Martin Munro and Celia Britton, editors. Liverpool UP, 2012. 77–94.

Lowe, John Wharton. *Calypso Magnolia: The Crosscurrents and Caribbean and Southern Literature.* U of North Carolina P, 2016.

Malcolm, X. *By Any Means Necessary; Speeches, Interviews, and a Letter,* George Brietman, ed. Pathfinder Press, 1970.

Mao, Douglas and Rebecca L. Walkowitz. *Bad Modernisms.* Duke UP, 2006.

——. "The New Modernist Studies." *PMLA* 123.3 (2008): 737–738.

Maxwell, William J. *New Negro, Old Left: African-American Writing and Communism Between the Wars.* Columbia UP, 1999.

McKay, Claude. *Harlem Shadows.* Harcourt, Brace and Company, 1922.

Mejías-López, Alejandro. *The Inverted Conquest: The Myth of Modernity and the Transatlantic Onset of Modernism.* Vanderbilt UP, 2009.

Mercer, Kobena. "Diaspora Aesthetics and Visual Culture." *Black Cultural Traffic: Crossroads in Global Performance and Popular Culture.* Harry J. Elam, Jr., and Kennell Jackson, eds. Ann Arbor: U of Michigan P, 2005. 141–161.

Michaels, Walter Benn. *Our America: Nativism, Modernism, and Pluralism.* Duke UP, 1995.

Miller, Monica. *Slaves to Fashion: Black Dandyism and the Styling of Black Diasporic Identity.* Duke UP, 2009.

Molesworth, Charles, ed. *The Works of Alain Locke.* Oxford UP, 2012.

Morgan, Denise C. "Jack Johnson: Reluctant Hero of the Black Community." *Akron Law Review.* 32.3 (1999) 529–556.

Morrison, Toni. *Playing in the Dark: Whiteness and the Literary Imagination.* Harvard UP, 1992.

Munro, Martin and Celia Britton, editors. *American Creoles: The Francophone Caribbean and the American South.* Liverpool UP, 2012.

Naipaul, V. S. *A Turn in the South.* Alfred A. Knopf, 1989.

Nardi, Steven A. "The 'Colder Artifice': Pau Laurence Dunbar, Countee Cullen, and the Mask of Blackness" in *Behind the Masks of Modernism: Global and Transnational Perspectives,* Bonnie Roos and Andrew Reynolds, eds. U of Florida P, 2016: 115–134.

North, Michael. *The Dialect of Modernism: Race, Language, and Twentieth-Century Literature.* Oxford UP, 1994.

Novillo-Corvolán, Patricia. *Modernism and Latin America: Transnational Networks of Literary Exchange.* Routledge, 2018.

Omi, Michael and Howard Winant. *Racial Formation in the United States.* Routledge, 1986.

——. "The Theoretical Status of the Concept of Race." In *Race, Identity, and Representation in Education* (second edition), edited by Cameron McCarthy, Warren Crichlow, Greg Dimitriadis, and Nadine Dolby, 3–12. Routledge, 2005.

Orwell, George. *Burmese Days*. Harper & Brothers, 1934.

Painter, Nell Irvin. *The History of White People*. W. W. Norton & Co., 2010.

Parker, Andrew and Eve Kosofsky Sedgwick, eds., *Performativity and Performance*. Routledge, 1995.

Phillips, Ruth B. "Aesthetic Primitivism Revisited: The Global Diaspora of 'Primitive Art' and the Rise of Indigenous Modernisms." *Journal of Art Historiography*. vol. 12 (June 2015): 1–25.

Platt, Lenn, ed. *Modernism and Race*. Cambridge UP, 2011.

Pollard, Charles W. *New World Modernisms: T.S. Eiot, Derek Walcott, Kamau Brathwaite*. UP of Virginia, 2004.

Pound, Ezra. *Selected Letters of Ezra Pound, 1907-1941*. D. D. Paige, ed. New Directions Publishing, 1971.

Puri, Shalini. *The Caribbean Postcolonial: Social Equality, Post-Nationalism, and Cultural Hybridity*. Palgrave Macmillan, 2004.

Ramazani, Jahan. *Poetry of Mourning: The Modern Elegy from Hardy to Heaney*. U of Chicago P, 1994.

Rampersad, Arnold. *The Art and Imagination of W.E.B. Du Bois*. Harvard, 1976.

____. *The Life of Langston Hughes, Volumes I and II*. Oxford UP, 186, 1988.

Reid-Pharr, Robert. "Engendering *The Black Atlantic*." *Found Object*. 4 (1994): 11–16.

Rice, Edward Le Roy. *Monarchs of Minstrelsy, from "Daddy" Rice to Date*. New York: Kenny Publishing Company, 1911.

Romine, Scott. *The Real South: Southern Narrative in the Age of Cultural Reproduction*. Louisiana State UP, 2008.

Said, Edward. *Orientalism*. Pantheon Books, 1978.

Scheper, Jeanne. *Moving Performances: Divas, Iconicity, and Remembering the Modern Stage*. Rutgers UP, 2016.

Schmidt, Peter. *Sitting in Darkness: New South Fiction, Education, and the Rise of Jim Crow Colonialism, 1865-1920*. UP of Mississippi, 2008.

Seshagiri, Urmila. *Race and the Modernist Imagination*. Cornell UP, 2010.

Simpson, Lewis P. *The Man of Letters in New England and the South: Essays on the History of the Literary Vocation in America*. Louisiana State UP, 1973.

Smallwood, Stephanie. *Saltwater Slavery: A Middle Passage from Africa to American Diaspora*. Harvard UP, 2008.

Smethurst, James. *The African American Roots of Modernism: From Reconstruction to the Harlem Renaissance*. U of North Carolina P, 2011.

Sotiropoulos, Karen. *Staging Race: Black Performers in Turn of the Century America*. Cambridge: Harvard UP, 2006.

Southerners. *I'll Take My Stand: The South and the Agrarian Tradition*. Louisiana State UP, 1978.

Stein, Gertrude. *The Making of Americans*. Contact Press, 1925.

Stovall, Tyler. *Paris Noir: African Americans in the City of Light*. Houghton Mifflin, 1996.

Street, Susan Castillo, and Charles Crow, eds. *The Palgrave Handbook of the Southern Gothic*. Palgrave Macmillan, 2016.

Swindall, Lindsey R. *Paul Robeson: A Life of Activism and Art*. Rowman & Littlefield, 2013.

Thaggert, Miriam. *Images of Black Modernism: Verbal and Visual Strategies of the Harlem Renaissance*. U of Massachusetts P, 2010.

Toomer, Jean. *Cane*. Boni & Liveright, 1923.

Van Notten, Eleonore. *Wallace Thurman's Harlem Renaissance*. Rodopi, 1994.

Vogel, Shane. *The Scene of the Harlem Cabaret: Race, Sexuality, Performance*. U of Chicago P, 2009.

Walker, Alice. "In Search of Our Mothers' Gardens: The Creativity of Black Women in the South." *Ms*. 1974.

———. *In Search of Our Mothers' Gardens: Womanist Prose*. Harcourt Brace Jovanovich, 1983.

Ward, Abigail Lara, ed. *Postcolonial Traumas: Memory, Narrative, Resistance*. Palgrave Macmillan, 2013.

Ware, Vron. *Beyond the Pale: White Women, Racism, and History*. Verso, 1992.

Watts, Sheldon. *Epidemics and History: Disease, Power, and Imperialism*. Yale UP, 1997.

Wells, Jeremy. *Romances of the White Man's Burden: Race, Empire, and the Plantation in American Literature, 1880-1936*. Vanderbilt UP, 2011.

Welsch, Tricia. "Killing Them with Tap Shoes." *Journal of Popular Film & Television*. 25.4 (1998): 162–171.

Wiedorn, Michael. "Go Slow Now: Saying the Unsayable in Édouard Glissant's Reading of Faulkner." *American Creoles: The Francophone Caribbean and the American South*. Edited by Martin Munro and Celia Britton. Liverpool UP, 2012. 183–196.

Will, Barbara. *Gertrude Stein, Modernism, and the Problem of "Genius."* Edinburgh UP, 2000.

Williams, John Frank. *The Quarantined Culture: Australian Reactions to Modernism, 1913-1939*. Cambridge UP, 1995.

Willmott, Glenn. *Modernist Goods: Primitivism, The Market and The Gift*. U of Toronto P, 2008.

Wilson, James F. *Bulldaggers, Pansies, and Chocolate Babies: Performance, Race, and Sexuality in the Harlem Renaissance*. U of Michigan P, 2010.

Woodward, C. Vann. *The Burden of Southern History*. Louisiana State UP, 1960, 1993.

Woolfe, Virginia. *Orlando: A Biography*. Hogarth P, 1928.

Wright, Richard. Rev. of *Their Eyes Were Watching God*. *New Masses*. (Oct. 5, 1937): 22–23.

Young, Robert J. C. *Colonial Desire: Hybridity in Theory, Culture and Race*. Routledge, 1995.

Young, Robert J. C. *Postcolonialism: An Historical Introduction*. Wiley-Blackwell, 2001.

WORKS CONSULTED

Abadie, Ann J. and Jay Watson, eds. *Faulkner's Geographies*. U of Mississippi P, 2015.

Abernathy, Jeff. *To Hell and Back: Race and Betrayal in the Southern Novel*. U of Georgia P, 2003.

Archer-Straw, Petrine. *Negrophilia: Avant-Garde Paris and Black Culture in the 1920s*. Thames & Hudson, 2000.

Arnold, James A. *Modernism and Negritude: The Poetry and Poetics of Amié Césaire*. Harvard College, 1981.

Artuso, Kathryn Stelmach. *Transatlantic Renaissances: Literature of Ireland and the American South*. U of Delaware P, 2013.

Ashcroft, Bill and John Salter. "Modernism's Empire: Australia and the Cultural Imperialism of Style" in *Modernism and Empire: Writing and British Coloniality 1890-1940*, Nigel Rigby and Howard J. Booth, eds. Manchester UP, 2000: 292–345.

Balshaw, Maria. "Black Was White: Urbanity, Passing and the Spectacle of Harlem." *Journal of American Studies*, vol. 33, (1999): 307–322.

Balthaser, Benjamin. *Anti-Imperialist Modernism: Race and Transnational Radical Culture from the Great Depression to the Cold War*. U of Michigan P, 2016.

Barkan, Elazar and Ronald Bush, et. al. *Prehistories of the Future: The Primitivist Project of the Culture of Modernism*. Stanford UP, 1995.

Bashford, Alison. *Imperial Hygiene: A Critical History of Colonialism, Nationalism, and Public Health*. Palgrave Macmillan, 2004.

Bennett, Lerone. "Jack Johnson and the Great White Hope." *Ebony* (April 1994): 86–98.

Berliner, Brett. *Ambivalent Desire: The Exotic Other in Jazz-Age France*. U of Massachusetts P, 2002.

Blake, Jody. *Le Tumulte Noir: Modernist Art and Popular Entertainment in Jazz-Age Paris, 1900-1930*. Pennsylvania State UP, 1999.

Blint, Rich. *Baldwin for Our Times: Writings from James Baldwin in a Time of Sorrow*. Beacon Press, 2016.

Bongie, Chris. *Islands and Exiles: The Creole Identities of Post/Colonial Literature*. Stanford UP, 1998.

Bornstein, George. "The Once and Future Texts of Modernist Poetry" in *The Future of Modernism*, Hugh Witemeyer, ed. U of Michigan Press, 1997: 161–179.

Briggs, Gabriel A. *The New Negro in the Old South*. Rutgers UP, 2015.

Brown, Jayna. *Babylon Girls: Black Women Performers and the Shaping of the Modern*. Duke UP, 2008.

Castillo, Susan Street and Charles Crow, eds. *The Palgrave Handbook of the Southern Gothic*. Palgrave, 2016.

Clukey, Amy and Jeremy Wells. *Global South: Special Issue: Plantation Modernity* Volume 10, Number 2 (Fall 2016).

Cordova, Ruben Charles. *Primitivism and Picasso's Early Cubism*. U of California P, 1998.

Cruse, Harold. *The Crisis of the Negro Intellectual*. Morrow, 1967.

Dash, Michael J. *The Other America: Caribbean Literature in a New World Context*. U of Virginia P, 1998.

Davidson, Adenike Marie. *The Black National Novel: Imagining Homeplaces in Early African American Literature*. Third World Press, 2008.

DeGrazia, Victoria and Ellen Furlough, *The Sex of Things: Gender and Consumption in Historical Perspective*. U of California P, 1996.

Dennis, Helen May. "Primitivism in Poundian Poetics: The Modernist Quest for Ancient Wisdom." *Ezra Pound, Ends and Beginnings: Essays and Poems from Ezra Pound International Conference*, John Pratt, ed. AMS, 2011: 97–199.

Dore, Florence. "The Modernism of Southern Literature." *A Concise Companion to American Fiction 1900-1950*, Peter Stoneley and Cindy Weinstein, eds. Blackwell, 2007: 228–252.

Doyle, Laura and Laura Winkiel, editors. *Geomodernisms: Race, Modernism, Modernity*. Indiana UP, 2005.

Duvall, John N. *Race and White Identity in Southern Fiction: From Faulkner to Morrison*. Palgrave MacMillan, 2008.

Ewing, Adam. *The Age of Garvey: How a Jamaican Activist Created a Mass Movement and Changed Global Black Politics*. Princeton UP, 2014.

Folks, Jeffrey J. *From Richard Wright to Toni Morrison: Ethics in Modern & Postmodern American Narrative*. Peter Lang, 2001.

Forter, Greg. *Gender, Race, and Mourning in American Modernism*. Cambridge UP, 2011.

Gaines, Malik. *Black Performance on the Outskirts of the Left: A History of the Impossible*. NYU Press, 2017.

Gardner, Sarah E. *Reviewing the South: The Literary Marketplace and the Southern Renaissance, 1920-1941*. Cambridge UP, 2017.

Geggus, David P, editor. *The Impact of the Haitian Revolution in the Atlantic World*. U of South Carolina P, 2001.

Gerzina, Gretchen. *Black England: Life Before Emancipation*. Allison and Busby, 1995.

Gottschild, Brenda Dixon. *The Black Dancing Body: A Geography From Coon to Cool*. Palgrave Macmillan, 2003.

____. *Waltzing in the Dark: African American Vaudeville and Race Politics in the Swing Era*. Palgrave, 1999.

Graham, Shane. "Cultural Exchange in a Black Atlantic Web: South African Literature, Langston Hughes, and Negritude." *Twentieth Century Literature* vol. 60, no. 4. (Winter 2014): 481–512.

Grant, Nathan. *Masculinist Impulses: Toomer, Hurston, Black Writing, and Modernity*. U of Missouri P, 2004.

Gray, Jonathan W. *Civil Rights in the White Literary Imagination: Innocence by Association*. U of Mississippi P, 2013.

Hakutani, Yoshinobu. *Cross-Cultural Visions in African American Modernism: From Spatial Narrative to Jazz Haiku*. Ohio State UP, 2006.

Henderson, Mae G. *Josephine Baker and Le Revue Négre*. Oxford UP, 2014.

Huddle, Marl Andrew. "Harlem, the 'New Negro,' and the South: History of the Politics of Place." *Safundi*, vol. 9, no. 3, Jul. 2008. pp. 257–270.

Izenberg, Gerald N. *Identity: The Necessity of a Modern Idea*. U of Pennsylvania P, 2016.

Johnson, James Weldon. *The Autobiography of an Ex-Colored Man*. Sherman, French & Company, 1912.

Jones, Sharon L. *Rereading the Harlem Renaissance: Race, Class, and Gender in the Fiction of Jessie Fauset, Zora Neale Hurston, and Dorothy West*. Greenwood Publishing Group, 2002.

Joyce, Justin A, et al. "Baltimore is Still Burning: The Rising Relevance of James Baldwin." *James Baldwin Review* vol. 1, 2015, pp. 1–9.

Junyk, Ihor. *Foreign Modernism: Cosmopolitanism, Style, and Identity in Paris*. U of Toronto P, 2013.

Kraut, Anthea. "Between Primitivism and Diaspora: The Dance Performances of Josephine Baker, Zora Neale Hurston, and Katherine Dunham." *Theatre Journal*, vol. 55, no. 3, (Oct. 2003): 433–450.

Krasner, David. *A Beautiful Pageant: African American Theatre, Drama, and Performance in the Harlem Renaissance, 1910-1927*. Palgrave Macmillan, 2004.

Ladoo, Harold Sonny. *No Pain Like This Body*. House of Anansi Press, Ltd., 1972.

Larsen, Nella. *Passing*. Afred A. Knopf, 1929.

Lears, T. J. Jackson. *No Place of Grace: Antimodernism and the Transformation of American Culture, 1880-1920*. U of Chicago P, 1981.

Leighten, Patricia. "The White Peril and L'Arte Négre: Picasso, Primitivism, and Anticolonialism." In *Race-ing Art History: Critical Readings in Race and Art History*. Kymberly Pinder, ed. Routledge, 2002: 233–260.

Lynskey, Dorian. *33 Revolutions per Minute: A History of Protest Songs, from Billie Holiday to Green Day*. New York: Ecco, 2011.

Mathews, Donald G. "Lynching Is Part of the Religion of Our People: Faith in the Christian South," in *Religion in the American South: Protestants and Others in History and Culture*. Beth Barton Schweiger and Donald G. Mathews, eds. The U of North Carolina P, 2004. 153–194.

Matthews, John T. *William Faulkner: Seeing Through the South*. Wiley-Blackwell, 2009.

Maxwell, William J. "Born-Again, Seen-Again James Baldwin: Post-Postracial Criticism and the Literary History of Black Lives Matter." *American Literary History*, vol. 28, no. 4, (Winter 2016): 812–827.

McIvor, David W. "The Struggle of Integration: James Baldwin and Melanie Klein in the Context of Black Lives Matter." *James Baldwin Review*, vol. 2, (2016): 75–96.

McKay, Claude. *Harlem Shadows*. Harcourt, Brace and Co., 1922.

McWilliams, Susan J, et al. "James Baldwin and Black Lives Matter." *A Political Companion to James Baldwin*. UP of Kentucky, 2017: 361–372.

Munro, Martin and Celia Britton, editors. *American Creoles: The Francophone Caribbean and the American South*. Liverpool UP, 2012.

Nicholls, Peter. "African American Modernism." *Modernisms: A Literary Guide*. Palgrave Macmillan, 2009.

Novillo-Corvolán, Patricia. *Modernism and Latin America: Transnational Networks of Literary Exchange*. Routledge, 2018.

Oforlea, Aaron Ngozi. *James Baldwin, Toni Morrison, and the Rhetorics of Black Male Subjectivity*. Ohio State UP, 2017.

Page, Kezia Ann. *Transnational Negotiations in Caribbean Diasporic Literature: Remitting the Text*. Routledge, 2011.

Panish, Jon. *The Color of Jazz: Race and Representation in Postwar American Culture*. U of Mississippi P, 1997.

Patterson, Anita. *Race, American Literature and Transnational Modernism*. Cambridge UP, 2008.

Pavlic, Edward M. *Crossroads Modernism: Descent and Emergence in African-American Literary Culture*. U of Minnesota P, 2002.

Pavloska, Susanna. *Modern Primitives: Race and Language in Gertrude Stein, Ernest Hemingway, and Zora Neale Hurston*. Garland, 2000.

Perucci, Tony. *Paul Robeson and the Cold War Performance Complex: Race, Madness, Activism*. U of Michigan P, 2012.

Ponce, Martin Joseph. "Langston Hughes's Queer Blues." *Modern Language Quarterly*, vol. 66, (2005): 505–537.

Posnock, Ross. *Color & Culture: Black Writers and the Making of the Modern Intellectual*. Harvard UP, 1998.

"Prolegomena to Jesse Owens: American Ideas about Race and Olympic Races from the 1890s to the 1920s." *The International Journal of the History of Sport*, vol. 25, no. 2 (Feb. 2008): 224–246.

Rabaka, Reiland. *The Negritude Movement: W.E.B. DuBois, Leon Damas, Aimé Cesare, Leopold Senghor, Frantz Fanon, and the Evolution of an Insurgent Idea.* Lexington Books, 2015.

Rae, Hugh C. *The Savage and the City in the Work of T.S. Eliot.* Oxford UP, 1987.

Roos, Bonnie and Andrew Reynolds. *Behind the Masks of Modernism: Global and Transnational Perspectives.* U of Florida P, 2016.

Rowe, John Carlos. *Afterlives of Modernism: Liberalism, Transnationalism, and Political Critique.* Dartmouth College P, 2011.

Scott, Rebecca J. "Fault Lines, Color Lines, and Party Lines: Race, Labor, and Collective Action in Louisiana and Cuba, 1869-1912." in *Beyond Slavery: Explorations of Race, Labor, and Citizenship in Postemancipation Societies.* Frederick Cooper et al, eds. U of North Carolina P, 2000: 60–106.

Scruggs, Charles. "Looking for a Place to Land: Hemingway's Ghostly Presence in the Fiction of Richard Wright, James Baldwin, and Ralph Ellison." in *Hemingway and the Black Renaissance.* Charles Scruggs and Gary Edwards, eds. Ohio State UP, 2012.

See, Sam. "'Spectacles in Color: The Primitive Drag of Langston Hughes." *PMLA*, vol. 124, no. 3. (May 2009): 798–816.

Shack, William A. *Harlem in Montmartre: A Paris Jazz Story Between the Great Wars.* U of California P, 2001.

Sharpley-Whiting, Tracy. *Black Venus: Sexualized Savages, Primal Fears, and Primitive Narratives in French.* Duke UP, 1999.

____. *Bricktop's Paris: African American Women in Paris Between the Two World Wars.* SUNY P, 2015.

____. *Negritude Women.* U of Minnesota P, 2002.

Sidbury, James. *Becoming African in America: Race and Nation in the Early Black Atlantic.* Oxford UP, 2007.

Sullivan-Gonzalez, Douglass and Charles Reagan Wilson, editors. *The South and the Caribbean Essays and Commentaries.* UP of Mississippi, 2001.

Sweeney, Carole. *From Fetish to Subject: Race, Modernism, and Primitivism, 1919-1935.* Praeger, 2004.

Toninato, Paola and Robin Cohen, eds. *The Creolization Reader: Studies in Mixed Identities and Cultures.* Routledge, 2010.

Trombold, John. "The Minstrel Show Goes to the Great War: Zora Neale Hurston's Mass Cultural Other." *MELUS*, vol. 24, no. 1 (Spring 1999): 85–107.

Van Vechten, Carl. *Nigger Heaven.* Alfred A. Knopf, 1926.

Vincent, Ted *Keep Cool: The Black Activists Who Built the Jazz Age.* Pluto Press, 1995.

Wallace, Michelle. "Modernism, Post-Modernism, and the Problem of the Visual in Afro- American Culture." *Aesthetics in a Feminist Perspective*, edited by Hilde Hein and Carolyn Korsmeyer. U of Indiana P, 1993. 205–217.

Watson, Jay and James G. Thomas. *Faulkner and the Black Literatures of America*. U of Mississippi P, 2016.

Wiegman, Robyn. *American Anatomies: Theorizing Race and Gender*. Duke UP, 1995.

Wilks, Jennifer M. *Race, Gender, and Comparative Black Modernism: Suzanne Lasacade, Marita Bonner, Suzanne Césaire, Dorothy West*. Louisiana State UP, 2008.

Williams, Rosalind. *Dream Worlds: Mass Consumption in Late Nineteenth Century France*. U of California P, 1982.

Winkiel, Laura. *Modernism, Race and Manifestos*. Cambridge UP, 2008.

Witemeyer, Hugh, ed. *The Future of Modernism*. U of Michigan Press, 1997.

Wollaeger, Mark A. and Matt Eatough, eds. *The Oxford Handbook of Global Modernisms*. Oxford UP, 2012.

Woodward, C. Vann. *Origins of the New South, 1877-1913*. Louisiana State UP, 1951, 1981.

Young, Robert. *Signs of Race in Poststructuralism: Toward a Transformative Theory of Race*. UP of America, 2009.

INDEX